General Editor:	David Jollands
Design Director:	Elwyn Blacker
Consultant Authors:	Roy Edwards
	Alan Hibbert
	Jim Hudson
	John Little
	John Mason
	Cleland McVeigh
	Peter Metcalfe
	Beverley Moody
	Patrick Moore
	Keith Porter
	Tim Pridgeon
	Derek Slack
	Ian Soden
	Tony Soper
	Alan Thomas
Research Editor:	Simon Jollands
Design and Production:	BLA Publishing Limited
	Michael Blacker
	Simon Blacker
	Margaret Hickey
	Graeme Little
	Alison Lawrenson
Artists:	Paul Doherty
	Hayward & Martin
	Dennis Knight
	Richard Lewis
	Steve Lings/Linden Artists
	Eric Thomas
	Rosie Vane-Wright

SCIENCE UNIVERSE SERIES

EXPLORING SPACE AND ATOMS

ARCO PUBLISHING, INC.
NEW YORK

Acknowledgements

The publishers wish to thank the following organizations for their invaluable assistance in the preparation of this book.

British Telecom
Canon (UK)
Central Electricity Generating Board
Ford Motor Company
Kodak Museum
NASA
National Film Board of Canada
Philips International
Royal Greenwich Observatory
Royal Smeets Offset
Shell
Sony (UK)
Southern Positives and Negatives (SPAN)
Standard Telephones and Cables
United Nations Organization
US Information Service

Published by Arco Publishing, Inc.
215 Park Avenue South, New York, N.Y. 10003

© BLA Publishing Limited 1984

First published 1984

Library of Congress Cataloging in Publication Data

Main entry under title:

Exploring space and atoms

(Science universe series; v. 1)

Includes index.
Summary: Briefly discusses stars, planets, spaceships, elements, carbon, plastics, atoms, radioactivity, and other aspects of space and chemistry.

1. Astronomy – Juvenile literature. 2. Atoms – Juvenile literature. 3. Outer space – Exploration – Juvenile literature. 4. Chemistry – Juvenile literature. [1. Astronomy. 2. Atoms. 3. Outer space – Exploration. 4. Chemistry]

I. Arco Publishing   II. Series

QB46.E93 1984   500   83-26623
ISBN 0-668-06175-8

This book was designed and produced by
BLA Publishing Limited, Swan Court,
East Grinstead, Sussex, England.
A member of the Ling Kee Group
LONDON · HONG KONG · TAIPEI · NEW YORK · SINGAPORE

Phototypeset in Great Britain by
Southern Positives and Negatives (SPAN).
Color origination by Chris Willcock Reproductions and Premier Graphics.
Printed and bound in The Netherlands by
Royal Smeets Offset BV, Weert.

Photographic credits

t = top   *b* = bottom   *l* = left   *r* = right   *c* = centre

Cover photographs: *tl* NASA; *tc, tr* ZEFA; *bl* Biophoto Associates/NHPA; *br* Institute of Geological Sciences/NASA.

4, 5 Patrick Moore Picture Library; 6, 7*tl* Ann Ronan Picture Library; 7*tr* Michael Holford/Science Museum; 8*tr* Patrick Moore Picture Library; 8*b* Science Museum; 9*l* Patrick Moore Picture Library; 9*r* Mary Evans Picture Library; 10 Royal Greenwich Observatory; 11 Patrick Moore Picture Library; 12*t*, 12*b* Royal Greenwich Observatory; 13*t*, 13*b*, 14*l* Patrick Moore Picture Library/NASA; 14*r* Institute of Geological Sciences/NASA; 15*t*, 15*l* NASA; 16, 17*t* Institute of Geological Sciences/NASA; 17*b* Michael Holford; 19*t*, 19*c* Royal Greenwich Observatory; 19*b* ZEFA; 20/21*t*, 21*b*, 22/23 Royal Greenwich Observatory; 23*t* Mansell Collection; 23*b*, 24, 25*t*, 25*b* Patrick Moore Picture Library; 26*l*, 26*c*, 27*t*, 27*b* NASA; 27*r* ZEFA; 28*t* NASA; 28*b*, 29*t* Patrick Moore Picture Library/NASA; 29*c*, 29*b*, 29*r* NASA; 30*l* US Information Service/NASA; 30*r*, 31*tl*, 31*tr*, 31*bl* NASA; 31*br* ZEFA/NASA; 32*l* NASA; 32*t* Space Frontiers; 33*tl*, 33*bl* US Information Service/NASA; 33*br*, 35 Space Frontiers; 36*t* ZEFA; 36*b* Michael Holford/British Museum; 37, 38*l*, 38*t*, 38*tr* Mansell Collection; 39 Paul Brierley; 40, 41 Ann Ronan Picture Library; 42, 44*t* Alan Thomas; 44*b* Michael Holford; 45, 48 ZEFA; 50*l* Sarah Scott; 50*b* Stephen Dalton/NHPA; 51*l* Douglas Dickins/NHPA; 51*r* Barry Finch; 52 Mansell Collection; 53*t* Paul Brierley; 53*b* National Film Board of Canada; 54*l* United Kingdom Atomic Energy Authority; 55*r* Mansell Collection; 56*l* Mary Evans Picture Library/Sigmund Freud; 56*r* Central Electricity Generating Board; 57 ZEFA; 58, 59*l* Paul Brierley; 59*r* ZEFA; 60*tl* Patrick Moore Picture Library; 60*br* NASA; 61*bl* NASA; 61*tl*, 61*tr* ZEFA.

Conversion table for units

Length

1 nanometer (nm)	= 0.000001 millimeter	= 0.000000001 meter (one-billionth of a meter)
1 millimeter (mm)	= 0.1 centimeter	= 0.03937 inch
1 centimeter (cm)	= 10 millimeters	= 0.3937 inch
1 meter (m)	= 100 centimeters	= 39.37 inches
1 kilometer (km)	= 1000 meters	= 3280.8 feet = 0.621 mile

Area

1 square kilometer = 0.3861 square mile

Capacity

1 liter = 1.0567 quarts

Volume

1 cubic centimeter (cc) = 0.06102 cubic inch

Weight

1 kilogram (kg)	= 2.2 pounds	
1 metric ton	= 1000 kilograms	= 1.1 US tons

Contents

NOTE TO THE READER: while you are reading this book you will notice that certain words appear in **bold type**. This is to indicate a word listed in the Glossary on page 62. This glossary gives brief explanations of words which may be new to you.

Introduction

THE EARTH is our home in space. To us, it seems so important that it is not easy to realize that it is nothing more than a very small world in a very large universe. Early humans believed the Earth to be flat, with the Sun, Moon and stars moving round it once a day, and there was no reason for our distant ancestors to think otherwise. Yet today we know better, and we are fairly certain that we have drawn up a good picture of how the universe is arranged.

One thing we must become used to in studying astronomy is the idea of tremendous distances and tremendous periods of time. Walk a mile, and it seems a long way. Go on a flight from England to Australia and you will cover many thousands of miles. Astronomically, distances of this kind are very small indeed. The Moon, which is the closest body in space, moves round the Earth at a distance of about 380,000 km, while the distance of the Sun is about 150 million km.

It is not surprising that before the age of modern science, distances of this kind were quite impossible to understand. The same is true of time-measurement. A year seems a long time; but the age of the Earth is about 4.7 billion years, and the universe itself is very much older still.

In learning about astronomy a number of terms will be used over and over again. The first is a measurement of distance called the **light-year.** Light does have a definite velocity. It moves at about 300,000 km every second. This means that a ray of light can travel from the Earth to the Moon in only 1.25 seconds and light from the Sun only takes just over eight minutes to reach us. When you look at the Sun you are actually seeing it as it used to be eight minutes ago. In one year, light can travel about 9.5 thousand billion kilometers, and this distance is known as the light-year. Note that a light-year is a measurement of distance, not of time.

Look up into the sky on a clear night, and you will see many hundreds of stars. Each of these stars is a sun. Our Sun, which seems so brilliant to us, is nothing more than an ordinary star. We

The Great Spiral Galaxy in Andromeda. This is thought to be 2.2 million light-years away from us.

4

When a time exposure of the night sky is taken, with the camera pointing in the direction of the Pole Star, the stars appear to be moving in a circle. The pattern is due to the fact that the Earth is rotating on its axis. It is not the stars that are moving, but the Earth itself.

The Sun and the nine planets compared, with the sizes to the same scale. The Sun is so large in comparison to the planets that only a small part of it can be shown.

know of stars which are thousands of times more powerful than the Sun. They look so small and cool only because they are much further away. Even the nearest star lies at a distance of over four light-years, and the star-system of which the Sun is a member is about 100,000 light-years across.

Our own star system is called the **Galaxy.** However, it is not the only one. Telescopes can show us millions of others, and there are even a few which can be seen with the naked eye. The distances of the galaxies from Earth amount to millions or even billions of light-years.

The next term which is used frequently in the study of astronomy is the **solar system.** This is the system of which the Sun is the center. Round the Sun move nine planets, of which the Earth is one. There are also some less important bodies such as **comets**, which are made up mainly of gas and dust. Some of the planets have moons or **satellites** moving round them. The Earth has one such satellite, our Moon, which is smaller than the Earth. The Moon and the planets have no light of their own. They simply reflect the light of the Sun.

Human beings have always wanted to 'find out'. At first astronomers could do no more than look upward and try to explain what they saw. Then telescopes were invented, and in our own time we have been able to send spaceships to the Moon and some of the planets. We have found out a great deal, but there is still much that we do not know. So let us go back to the beginning, and trace the story from ancient times up to the present day.

5

The first star watchers

ASTRONOMY is probably the oldest of all the sciences, and some of the old ideas sound very strange today. Early astronomers believed the Earth to be flat, but this should not surprise us. After all, it does look flat, apart from nearby hills or valleys. The first astronomers also thought that the Sun and all the other bodies in the sky moved round the Earth.

In India it was thought that the Earth was lying on top of twelve tall pillars, so that during the hours of darkness the Sun had to pass underneath the Earth without hitting any of the pillars. Another idea was that the Earth stood on the back of four elephants. The elephants in turn stood on the back of a huge tortoise which was swimming in an ocean. The Chinese drew maps of the stars, and even worked out a calendar of 365 days, which is of course quite correct even though the Chinese did not believe that it was the Earth which was moving round the Sun.

Real astronomy began in Greece, and the first of the great Greek astronomers was Thales, who lived 600 years BC. By then, astronomers had divided the stars up into patterns or **constellations**, and we still use these constellation pat-terns today, for example the Great Bear, Orion, and others. Thales was wrong in believing the Earth to be flat and motionless, and also wrong in thinking that all the stars lay at the same distance from us, but at least a start had been made.

At an early period it was also found that while the constellations always looked the same, there were some star-like bodies which moved slowly about from one constellation into another. These were the planets. Five of them were found, known to us today as Mercury, Venus, Mars, Jupiter and Saturn. Their movement was easy to see because they are members of the solar system, and much closer to Earth than the stars.

The next important step was the discovery that the Earth is not flat, but is a globe. About 280BC the Greek astronomer Eratosthenes proved this in a very clever way. He knew that at midday, in the middle of the summer, the Sun was exactly overhead as seen from the town of Syene, where he lived. However, at this same moment the Sun was not overhead at the town of Alexandria, some way along the Nile. From Alexandria, the Sun was then seven degrees

Eratosthenes' method of measuring the distance round the Earth *(bottom left)*. At noon the Sun was directly overhead at Syene and its rays shone directly into a well without casting a shadow. At Alexandria at the same time the Sun was 7° from the overhead point. He was therefore able to work out that the distance round the Earth would be about fifty times the distance between Syene and Alexandria.

Ptolemy's system of the Universe, showing the Earth surrounded by water, air and fire.

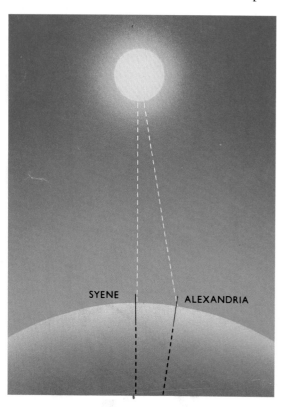

SYENE · ALEXANDRIA

Ptolemy using a quadrant for measuring the angle of the stars. Behind him stands Urania, the Muse of Astronomy. From an old print.

The Arabs were great astronomers. They used instruments like this astrolabe for calculating the position of the Sun, Moon and stars. An astrolabe is a model of the heavens. The word comes from the Greek and means 'star-taker'.

from the overhead point. A full circle contains 360 degrees, and seven is about one-fiftieth of 360. Therefore, if the Earth were a globe its circumference – that is to say, the distance all round it – would be fifty times the distance from Alexandria to Syene. Eratosthenes measured this distance and could then work out a value for the Earth's circumference. His answer was very nearly right. We know today that the circumference of the Earth is about 40,000 km.

Ptolemy believed that a planet moved in a small circle. The center of this small circle was itself moving round the Earth in a larger circle. Though this explanation was not correct it was generally accepted for some 1700 years.

Most of the Greek astronomers still believed that the Earth must be the center of the universe. The last great astronomer of ancient times, Ptolemy, wrote a book, about the year 150 BC, in which he described a system in which the Moon, the Sun, the planets and the stars all moved round the Earth in a period of twenty-four hours. He also believed that all the paths or **orbits** of the bodies in the sky must be exactly circular.

Little more was done for several hundreds of years after Ptolemy's death, but from about the year AD 813 great attention was paid to the sky by the Arabs. They drew up good star maps and even built **observatories**, though these observatories were very different from those of today. They contained no telescopes because these had not been invented.

Then, in 1543, a Polish astronomer named Copernicus put forward the idea that the Sun, not the Earth, was the center of the solar system. He knew that this would not be liked by the Church, because it meant that the Earth was not the most important body in the universe, and so he did not publish his book until just before he died. Indeed, it was not until a hundred years after his death that all astronomers had to admit that Ptolemy had been wrong, and Copernicus was right.

How the planets move

As soon as Copernicus' book had been published, an argument began between those who believed the Sun to be the center of the solar system and those who still thought the Earth to be the most important body in the universe. The Church was unfriendly to Copernicus' ideas and tried to prevent them from being accepted. One astronomer – Giordano Bruno – was burned at the stake in Rome in 1600 because he supported Copernicus. This was not Bruno's only crime in the eyes of the Church, but it was certainly an important one. The real truth was found in a rather unexpected way.

The greatest astronomer of the late sixteenth century was a Dane, Tycho Brahe. He was a hot-tempered man, and during his student days he had part of his nose cut off during a sword fight, so that he made himself a new one out of gold, silver and wax. He was an excellent observer and in 1576 he set up an observatory at Hven, an island in the Baltic Sea. Here he built measuring instruments with which he mapped the positions, not only of the stars, but also of the moving planets, particularly Mars. Tycho made very accurate measurements, but even so, he did not believe the Sun to be the center of the solar system. When he died in 1601 all his work was handed over to his last assistant, a German named Johannes Kepler.

Tycho Brahe, the Danish astronomer who made the first accurate observations of the stars.

Tycho and his assistants inside the observatory at Hven (right). The instruments were the best of their time and he obtained excellent results. He always dressed himself in special robes before observing the stars.

Tycho Brahe's great observatory at Hven where most of his work was done. Tycho left Denmark in 1596 and the observatory was never used again.

8

period is just over 365 days. Mercury, the closest planet to the Sun, takes only 88 days to complete its orbit. Neptune, the most distant of the main planets, takes over 164 years.

Kepler did not have a happy life; he was always in need of money, but at least he avoided trouble with the Church because he lived in Germany, where the laws were less strict than in some other countries.

Galileo, the other great astronomer of the time, was less lucky. He was a professor of mathematics in Italy, and early in his life he decided that Copernicus was right in saying that the Earth goes round the Sun. By 1609 the first telescopes had been made; Galileo built one himself, and used it to look at the Moon, planets and stars. He found that the lovely band of light

Galileo Galilei, the great Italian astronomer who was the first to use a telescope for observing the Moon and the stars.

Kepler made a very careful study of the wanderings of Mars, and at last he found the answer to the problems which had puzzled Tycho. Mars and the other planets, including the Earth, do move round the Sun, but their paths are not circular; they are **ellipses**. Once this discovery had been made, all Tycho's observations of Mars could be explained.

Between 1609 and 1618 Kepler published his Laws of Planetary Motion. The first of these states that a planet moves round the Sun in an ellipse, with the Sun at one **focus** of the ellipse. The second law states that a planet moves at its fastest when closest to the Sun, and slowest when it is furthest away. The third law gives a relationship between a planet's distance from the Sun and the time that it takes to complete one orbit. In the case of the Earth, of course, this

Drawing an ellipse. Fix two pins into a piece of board and join them with a loose thread as shown. Place a pencil through the thread and trace out a curve. This curve will be an ellipse, and the pins will mark the foci of the ellipse.

crossing the sky, which we call the Milky Way, was made up of countless stars. He also saw mountains and **craters** on the Moon and when he looked at Jupiter, the largest of the planets, he found that it had not one moon but four. These satellites moved round Jupiter, so that at least the Earth could not be the center of everything.

Galileo did not try to hide his opinions. He wrote them down in a great book, and this led to his being called to Rome and put on trial. He was even made to say publicly that he no longer believed in Copernicus' ideas, after which he was kept under close guard until he died in 1642. But by then most astronomers were sure that the Earth really does move round the Sun, even though some of them did not dare risk saying so.

Telescopes and Isaac Newton

THE TELESCOPE is certainly the most important of the instruments used by astronomers. Galileo's own telescopes were **refractors**, and were much less powerful than modern binoculars. Even so they caused a complete change in our ideas.

With a refracting telescope, the light from the body to be observed, the Moon for example, is collected by a glass **lens**, known as an **object-glass.** This lens is specially shaped, and bunches the rays of light together, bringing them to what is called the **focus.** Here, a second lens or eyepiece is placed to magnify the image which has been produced at the focus. The larger the object-glass, the more light can be collected. However, it is important to remember that the magnification is due to the eyepiece, and all telescopes are fitted with several eyepieces to give different magnifications.

Galileo's largest telescope could give a

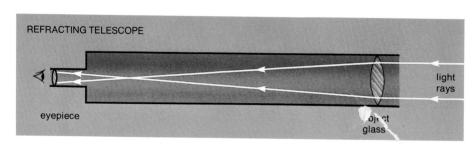

REFRACTING TELESCOPE

eyepiece

light rays

object glass

magnification of no more than 30, and the telescope could be held in the hand. The largest refractor in the world, at Yerkes Observatory in Wisconsin, has an object-glass of 101.6 cm diameter. It is set up in a large dome, with a revolving roof and a slit which can be opened when the telescope is to be used. Early refractors were difficult to use, because it was not known how to make a large, good quality object-glass. The next step was taken by Isaac Newton.

Newton was born in 1643, a year after

In a refracting telescope, called a refractor, the light is collected by a large lens *(right)*. This is known as the object-glass. It is focused on to another lens, or eyepiece, which magnifies the picture.

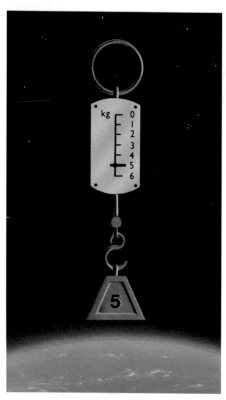

A 5-kg mass weighed on Earth shows 5 kg on the spring balance. The Earth's gravity pulls the mass downwards.

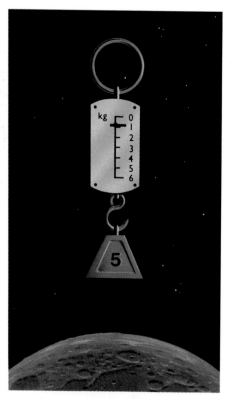

The same 5-kg mass weighed on the Moon shows slightly less than 1 kg on the spring balance. The Moon's gravity is one-sixth that of the Earth.

Galileo died, and spent much of his life in Cambridge, England. It was he who worked out the laws of gravitation upon which all modern astronomy is based. According to a story which is probably true, he was sitting in his garden when he saw an apple fall from a tree. He realized that the force which pulled down the apple was the same as the force which keeps the Moon in its path round the Earth. It is also the force which keeps the Earth in its path round the Sun. Every body attracts every other body. The reason why the Moon does not fall down to the Earth is because it is moving, and it keeps moving because there is nothing to stop it.

In 1687 Newton published his book, known to us as the *Principia*, in which he explained the laws of gravitation. He even explained the tides, which are caused by the pull of the Moon. The Moon tries to drag both the land and the sea toward it. However, water is more easily pulled than solid land so that it piles up to make a high tide.

Some years earlier Newton had made a completely different type of telescope, the **reflector.** His first reflector, shown to the Royal Society in 1671, had no object-glass. Instead the light travelled down an open-ended tube and

fell upon a curved mirror. This mirror sent the light back up the tube on to a smaller flat mirror, which sent the rays into the side of the tube. Here the focus was formed and the image magnified by an eyepiece as before. With a reflector of this type, you look into the side of the tube instead of up it.

Newton's first reflector had a mirror only 2.5 cm in diameter. The largest telescope of this kind in the world today is in Russia and has a 6-m mirror. Many modern telescopes have optical arrangements different from Newton's, but it was he who showed the way, and for most astronomical work a reflector is much more suitable than a refractor.

In a Newtonian reflector the light passes down an open tube and falls on to a large curved mirror *(left)*. The light is reflected back up the tube and is focused on to a smaller flat mirror set at an angle of 45°. The image is then magnified by an eyepiece set in the side of the tube. The viewer looks into the side of the tube and not up it.

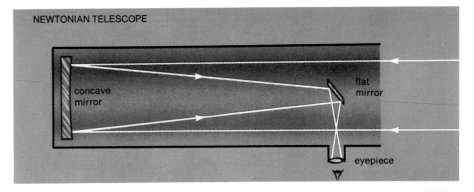

NEWTONIAN TELESCOPE

concave mirror

flat mirror

eyepiece

Part of the new international observatory at La Palma in the Canary Islands. The dome of the 2.5-m Isaac Newton telescope is to the right, and that of the 1-m telescope to the left of the picture.

The Anglo-Australian telescope. Light from the stars enters the reflector through an opening in the dome.

The Moon, our companion

ANY SMALL TELESCOPE will show the mountains and craters of the Moon. Even with the naked eye it is easy to see dark patches, which are still called 'seas' even though there has never been any water in them. Galileo used his tiny telescope to study the Moon, and even managed to make some fairly accurate measurements of the heights of the lunar mountains, which rise to over 6000 m in places.

Because the Moon has no light of its own, it shows regular **phases**, or apparent changes of shape. The Sun can light up only half of the Moon at any one time, so that when the Moon is almost between the Sun and the Earth its dark side is turned toward us and we cannot see it easily. This is called a new moon. If the new moon passes exactly between the Sun and the Earth it blots out the brilliant face of the Sun, and causes what is called a solar **eclipse**, but this does not happen at every new moon, because the Moon's path is tilted. Generally the new moon passes either above or below the Sun in the sky, and there is no eclipse.

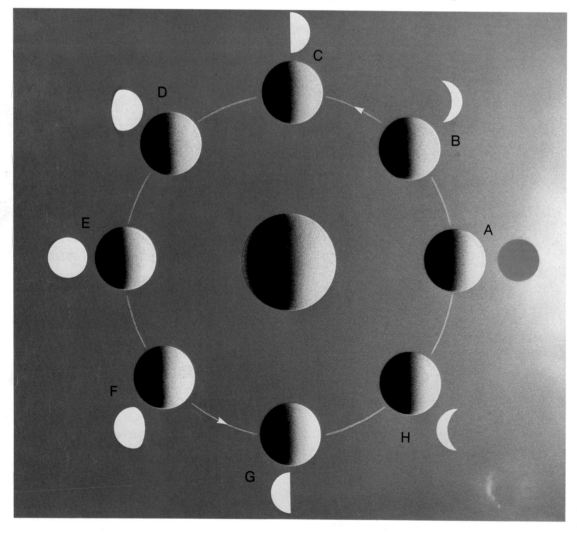

Half moon, showing its heavily cratered surface.

The phases of the Moon. In the picture, the Sun is shining from the right. In position A, the dark side of the Moon faces us. This is a new moon. Between A and C (half moon) it is crescent-shaped. Between C and E (full moon) it is gibbous. After full moon, it wanes through half moon (G) and crescent (H) to new moon again. This whole process takes 27.3 days.

As the Moon moves along, a little of the sunlit side begins to show; we have a **crescent**, then a half moon, and then full moon, with all the sunlit side facing us. After full, the Moon becomes a half again, and then a crescent, before reaching the new moon position once more. The Moon takes just over twenty-seven days to go round the Earth, so generally there is one new moon and one full moon every month.

Galileo knew the cause of the Moon's phases, and he made some drawings of the mountains and craters. Later, as better telescopes were made, more and more detail could be seen. The Moon is a world of craters, some of them well over 160 km in diameter and very deep. They may even have mountains in the centers of their floors.

The Moon is a small world, with a diameter of only 3476 km. It would take eighty-one Moons to weigh as much as the Earth, and for this reason the Moon's pull of gravity is not nearly so strong. One result of the weak gravity is that the Moon has no air, or atmosphere, which means that it can have no water and no life.

To show why the Moon has no atmosphere try a simple experiment. Take a solid object (a football, for instance) and throw it up gently. It will reach a certain height and then come down. Throw it up faster and it will rise higher. If you could throw it upward at a speed of 11.2 km per second, or about 40,000 km per hour, it would never come down at all. The Earth's gravity would not be able to draw it back and the ball would escape into space. This is why 11.2 km per second is called the Earth's **escape velocity.**

The air you breathe is made up of small **particles**, all flying around. They cannot break

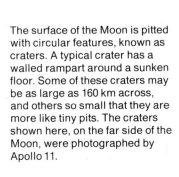

This photograph taken from the lunar module shows the Earth rising over the Moon's horizon. Like the Moon, the Earth has no light of its own. It reflects the light of the Sun and has phases, just as the Moon does.

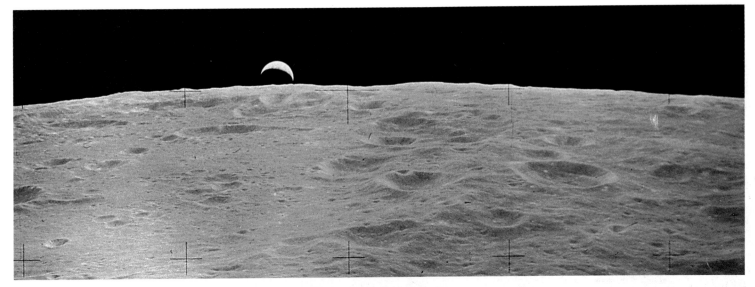

The surface of the Moon is pitted with circular features, known as craters. A typical crater has a walled rampart around a sunken floor. Some of these craters may be as large as 160 km across, and others so small that they are more like tiny pits. The craters shown here, on the far side of the Moon, were photographed by Apollo 11.

free because they cannot reach 11.2 km per second. However, the Moon's escape velocity is only 2.4 km per second, which is not enough. Any air the Moon may once have had has escaped into space, so that today the Moon has no atmosphere at all.

Another interesting fact is that the Moon spins round in just the same time that it takes to go once round the Earth: 27.3 days. This means that it keeps the same face toward us all the time. You can show this by walking round a chair, keeping your face turned to the chair all the time. Anyone sitting on the chair will never see the back of your neck. In the same way from the Earth we can never see the 'other side of the Moon'. By now spaceships, both manned and unmanned, have flown round the Moon, and we have good maps of the whole of the surface. The far side is just as cratered and just as lifeless as the side we can always see.

Exploring the planets

OF THE NINE PLANETS in the Sun's family, five – Mercury, Venus, Mars, Jupiter and Saturn – look like bright stars, so that they must have been seen by our earliest ancestors. The Earth comes third in order of distance from the Sun. Three more planets – Uranus, Neptune and Pluto – have been discovered in modern times.

Early telescopes could not show much on the planets, but at least astronomers knew how they moved. The solar system is divided into two parts. The inner part contains the four small planets, from Mercury to Mars. Then comes a wide gap, in which move thousands of tiny worlds known as minor planets or **asteroids**, and then follow the four giants. Pluto, the other distant body, is smaller than the Moon, and may not be a proper planet at all.

Using his telescope, Galileo could see that Mercury and Venus show phases like those of the Moon, and for much the same reason even though they move round the Sun and not round the Earth. Mercury is only 4 880 km in diameter, and is not easy to see. However, it is visible with the naked eye when low down in the west after sunset or low down in the east before sunrise. Venus is nearly as large as the Earth, and is very brilliant. It can even cast a shadow. Unfortunately no details can be seen on it, because it is always covered with a thick, cloudy atmosphere. Spacecraft have been sent there and we now know that Venus is a very unfriendly world, with a surface temperature of about 500°C. It also has an unbreathable atmosphere, and clouds which contain a poisonous substance known as sulfuric acid.

(opposite) Io, seen here from Voyager 1, is the innermost of Jupiter's satellites. About the size of our Moon, it has a diameter of 3640 km.

(left) Mars. This picture shows the Viking 2 landing site some months after the craft had arrived. There are scattered rocks on the surface but no Martians.

(below) Bright clouds of water ice above the rust-coloured background of the Martian desert. The area shown is about 10,000 square kilometers.

Jupiter (left), with satellites Io and Europa, from Voyager 1. This photograph was taken about 28 million kilometers from the planet. The Great Red Spot is visible to the lower left of the planet's disk. Above it and to the right is the orange-colored satellite Io. Out to the right of Jupiter is the satellite Europa.

The planet Saturn (below) and some of its satellites. This picture was put together from a number of photographs taken by Voyager 1 in 1980. The satellite Dione in the foreground is 377,500 km from Saturn. The planet itself is vast and has a diameter nearly ten times that of the Earth.

of small pieces of ice spinning round the planet like tiny moons. Galileo saw that there was something strange about Saturn, but he could not make out what it was; the rings were discovered by a Dutch astronomer, Huygens, in the year 1656. Saturn has over twenty satellites. One of them, Titan, has a thick atmosphere, and there may be oceans on its surface, though these oceans do not contain water. They are more likely to be seas of a substance called **methane**.

Three spaceships have now been past Saturn. The best pictures have come from Voyager 1, in 1980, and Voyager 2 in 1981. Neither of these spacecraft will ever come back. They are on their way out of the solar system, and after we can no longer pick up their radio signals we will never know what finally happens to them.

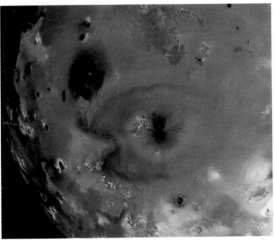

Mars, the first planet beyond the Earth's path round the Sun, looks like a bright red star. In size it is about half way between the Earth and the Moon. Telescopes show dark patches, while the poles are covered with white patches which contain large amounts of ordinary ice. Mars is more like the Earth than any other planet, but the unmanned spacecraft which have landed there have shown no sign of life.

Jupiter and Saturn are much further away. They have surfaces made of gas and inside they are mainly liquid, with solid centers. Both are very large. You could fit one thousand Earths inside Jupiter and still leave room to spare. Telescopes show dark belts on Jupiter, and also the four moons or satellites described by Galileo. Two of these satellites are much larger than our Moon, while another, Io, has a bright red surface with active volcanoes. From Earth, the satellites look like small stars. However, four spaceships have now been past Jupiter and have sent back pictures from close range.

Saturn, somewhat smaller than Jupiter, has a wonderful system of rings. These are made up

Discovering new worlds

SATURN was the most distant planet known in ancient times; it is 1.427 billion kilometers from the Sun and its orbital period or year is 29.5 times longer than Earth's. However, like Jupiter, it has a very short 'day' of less than eleven hours. The next planet, Uranus, was discovered in 1781 by an amateur astronomer named William Herschel, who earned his living by playing the organ in Bath, England. Herschel was charting the stars when he found something which could not be a star at all. Instead of looking like a dot of light, it appeared as a small greenish disc, and it moved slowly against the starry background from one night to the next. When its path was worked out, it was found to have a 'year' eighty-four times as long as ours, and to be much further away than Saturn.

Uranus is smaller than Jupiter or Saturn, with a diameter of only 51,800 km. It too has a surface made up of gas, and it has five satellites, all smaller than our Moon. It is just visible with the naked eye if you know where to look for it.

Before long, astronomers found that Uranus was not moving as had been expected. Something was pulling it out of position. Two astronomers, J. Adams in England and U. Le Verrier in France, decided that this 'something' must be another planet, well beyond Uranus. They worked out where the new planet should be and when telescopes were turned to that position in the sky, the planet was found almost at once. It was named Neptune, and is a little smaller than Uranus, though more massive. It is too faint to be seen without a telescope, and we can see no detail on its blue surface.

Still things were not quite right, and it seemed likely that yet another planet must exist. New measurements were made by an American astronomer, Percival Lowell, but for

This Voyager 2 picture *(right, above)* of Saturn's rings was taken from a distance of about 9 million km. The photograph tells a scientist that there are chemical differences from one part of the rings to another. A computer has been used to show these variations as false colors. The photograph seen here was put together from images taken through ultraviolet, clear and orange filters.

The Bayeux Tapestry *(right, below)*. Harold is told of Halley's comet. Can you find the comet in the picture?

Saturn *(below)* photographed from Voyager 1 on October 8, 1980. A special process, called color enhancing, has been used. This makes it easier to distinguish the large, bright features on Saturn's surface.

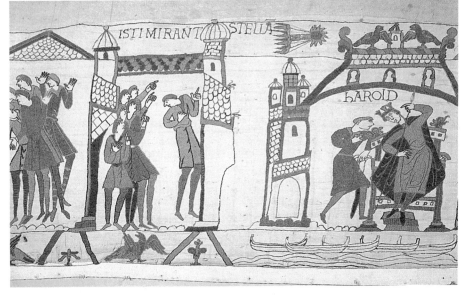

some time the expected planet could not be found. It was finally discovered in 1930, fourteen years after Lowell's death, by Clyde Tombaugh, using a telescope specially set up at Lowell's observatory in Arizona.

Pluto, as the new planet was named, is a puzzling world. It is smaller than the Moon and probably made up of a mixture of rock and ice. It has one satellite, Charon. When at its closest to the Sun it comes inside the orbit of Neptune, as is the case at the present time. However, it is so faint that a large telescope is needed to show it.

Pluto is so small that it could not possibly pull giant planets such as Uranus and Neptune out of position. The solar system contains bodies of other kinds. **Comets** are made up of thin gas and 'dust'; they move around the Sun, but usually in very stretched out paths. A large comet may have a long tail, which always points away from the Sun. Faint comets are common, but there is one bright comet, Halley's comet, which has a period of seventy-six years, so that we know when and where to expect it. It was last bright in 1910. In 1982 it was found again, and should be visible with the naked eye for some months between November 1985 and March 1986.

The smallest members of the Sun's family are the **meteors**. A meteor is a tiny object, usually smaller than a pin's head. When it dashes into the Earth's air, it is heated by rubbing against the atmosphere, and burns away in the streak of light which we call a shooting star. Many meteors travel around the Sun in swarms. Every time the Earth passes through a swarm, as happens several times each year, we see a shower of shooting stars. The best shower is that of early August. If you look up into a dark, clear sky any time between July 27 and August 17, you will probably see at least one shooting star.

The orbit of Halley's comet in the solar system.

Key to the diagram
A   1948: greatest distance
B   1977: crosses Uranus' orbit
C   1983: crosses Saturn's orbit
D   1985 *(summer)*: crosses Jupiter's orbit
E   1985 *(winter)*: crosses Mars' orbit
F   1986 (February): turns
G   1986 *(spring)*: crosses Mars' orbit
H   1986 *(autumn)*: crosses Jupiter's orbit
I   1988: crosses Saturn's orbit
J   1999: crosses Uranus' orbit

The comet should be visible to the naked eye between November 1985 and March 1986.

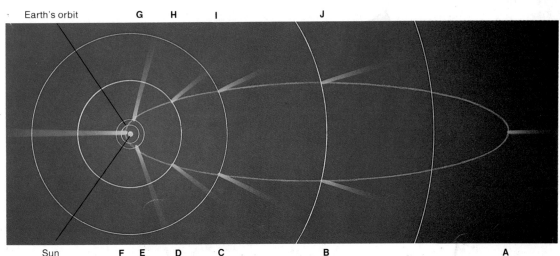

The Sun – our star

To us, the sun is the most important body in the sky. Without it we could not exist, and the Earth would not have been born. It is believed that the Earth and the other planets were formed over 4.5 billion years ago, from a cloud of material which then surrounded the young Sun.

The Sun is 1,392,000 km in diameter, and it is over one million times bigger than our Earth. It is made up of gas, and contains a vast amount of the lightest of all gases, **hydrogen.** Hydrogen is in fact the commonest substance in the whole universe. Water is made up of the two gases hydrogen and oxygen.

The Sun is very hot, with a surface temperature of 6 000°C, but it is not 'burning' in the usual meaning of the word. Deep inside it, where the temperatures are extremely high, hydrogen is being changed into another substance, called **helium.** Every time this happens a little energy is set free, and a little **mass,** or amount of material, is lost. It is this energy which keeps the Sun shining. The loss in mass is 4 million metric tons every second, so that the Sun's mass is much less now than it was when you started to read this page. Luckily the Sun is so large that it will not change much for at least 5 billion years in the future.

On the Sun's bright face, darker patches known as **sunspots** can often be seen, but a word of warning is needed here. Never look directly at the Sun either with the naked eye, or through a telescope, or even binoculars. The result will be to concentrate all the Sun's light and heat on to your eyes, and cause permanent blindness. Even using a dark glass in front of the telescope eyepiece is unwise. Dark glasses have a habit of cracking suddenly, and in any case they do not block out enough light and heat. There is only one good rule about looking straight at the Sun: *don't.*

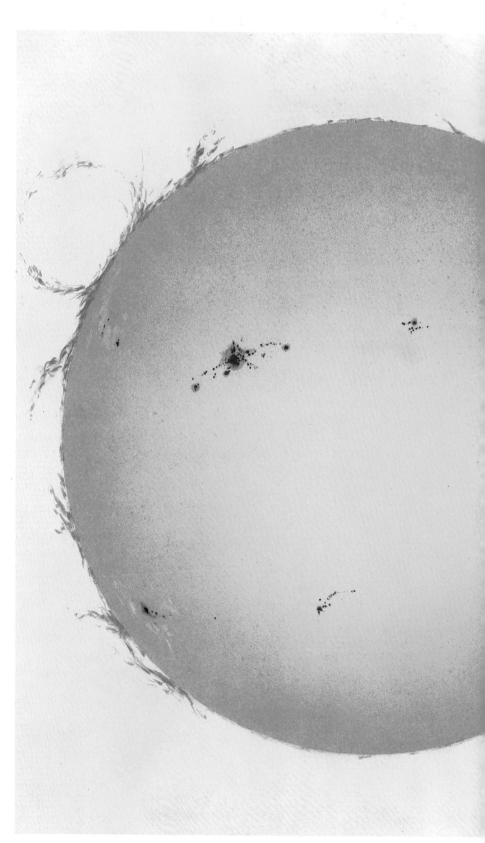

Though vast in size compared with our planet Earth, the Sun is no more than an ordinary star. Large sunspots can be as much as 100,000 km wide, but the normal diameter is about 10,000 km. The prominences are giant 'flames' extending many thousands of km from the Sun's surface.

A solar prominence (top left) and the inner corona photographed during the total eclipse of the Sun on May 29, 1929, from Sobral in Brazil.

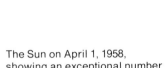

The Sun on April 1, 1958, showing an exceptional number of large sunspots.

Sunspots are not always on view, and no one spot lasts for more than a few weeks or months. Every eleven years the Sun is very active, with many spots. Activity then dies down, and there are years when very few spots are seen. The last really active period was in 1980, so that the next will probably be about 1991.

When the Moon passes in front of the Sun and causes an eclipse, the Sun's atmosphere can be seen – an inner red ring, and an outer pearly mist called the **corona**, which is made up of very thin gas. This can only be seen when the eclipse is total. Total eclipses are rare, from any one point on the Earth's surface. The last seen in the United States was in 1983, while the next will not be until the 1990s. If the Sun is only partly covered by the Moon, the corona cannot be seen.

Using special equipment, astronomers can now study the Sun's outer parts without waiting for an eclipse. Huge clouds of red hydrogen can be seen, and sometimes there are violent explosions called **flares.** The Sun is never calm and quiet. Yet we know that it is nothing more than an ordinary star and not nearly so powerful as many of the stars to be seen on any clear night.

This photograph of a solar prominence was taken from Skylab 3 using special equipment. The picture is reproduced in false color, the brighter colors showing hotter regions.

Earth

Distant stars

Look at a star through a telescope, and you will see nothing more than a dot of light. This is because the stars are so far away. As we have seen, even the closest star is more than four light-years from us. If we make a scale model, and let the distance between the Sun and the Earth be represented by 1 cm, the nearest star will be about 2.5 km away.

The first astronomer to measure the distance of a star was Friedrich Bessel, director of an observatory in Germany, in 1838. He succeeded in using the method which we now call **parallax**. This can be explained by a simple experiment. Close your right eye and hold out a finger, lining it up with a distant object such as a tree. Now, without moving your finger, close your left eye and open your right eye. The finger will no longer be lined up with the tree because you are looking at it from a slightly different direction. Your two eyes are not in the same place.

The apparent shift is a measure of your finger's parallax.

Bessel used this method, but he had to find a very long base-line – that is to say, a line joining the two places from which he was looking. He chose the Earth's orbit which has a diameter of about 300 million km and observed a faint star which he thought must be one of our closest neighbors. He measured the position of the star first in January and then in July, when the Earth had moved round to the other side of its orbit. He found a parallax shift, and was able to show that this star, 61 Cygni, was over ten light-years away.

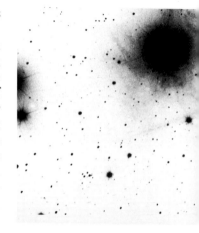

The parallax method of measuring star distances, used by Bessel. His values were almost as accurate as those accepted by astronomers today.

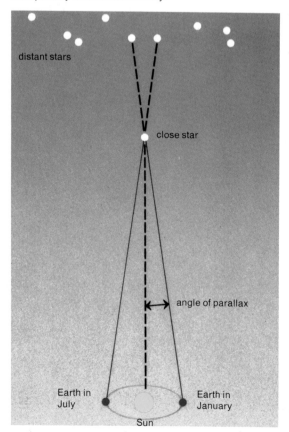

distant stars

close star

angle of parallax

Earth in July

Earth in January

Sun

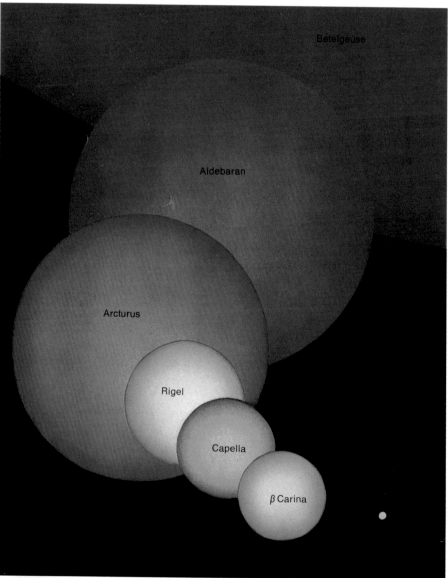

Betelgeuse

Aldebaran

Arcturus

Rigel

Capella

β Carina

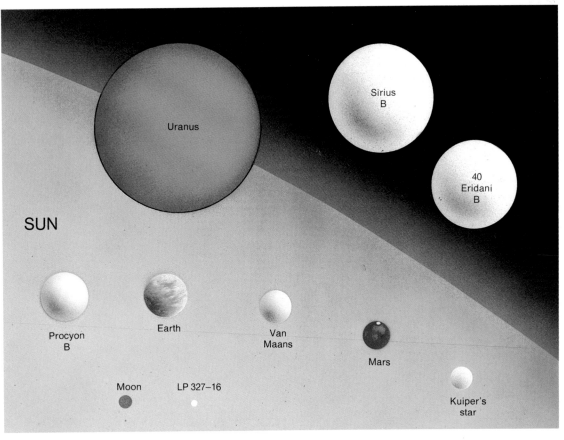

The Pleiades star cluster *(below)* in the constellation Taurus. The fuzzy streaks and patches are a result of starlight being scattered by dust particles in the cluster.

Some giant stars *(left)* compared with the Sun (the small white dot, bottom right). Betelgeuse is 1200 times as bright as the Sun. Its diameter is 400 million km.

With stars more than a few hundreds of light-years away, the parallax shifts become too small to be measured, and astronomers are forced to use less direct methods. Most of these depend upon what is called the **spectroscope.** Just as a telescope collects light, so a spectroscope splits light up, and can show what makes up the body which is shining. From this, it is often possible to tell how powerful a star really is, and this in turn tells us its distance. For example, Rigel in the constellation of Orion is about 900 light-years away. We are seeing it not as it is today, but as it used to be 900 years ago, in the time of William the Conqueror. Another bright star in Orion, Betelgeuse, is less than 500 light-years away. It is very important to remember that the stars in any particular constellation are not truly close together. They simply happen to lie in much the same direction as seen from Earth.

Betelgeuse is orange-red because its surface is cooler than that of the yellow Sun or the bluish-white Rigel, but to make up for this Betelgeuse is so large that it could span the whole path of the Earth round the Sun. It is what is called a **red giant** star. There are plenty of these. Antares in the Scorpion is another good example.

Ordinary stars shine in the same way as the Sun, but not all stars end their lives in the same way. When the Sun has used up all its 'fuel', it will swell out and become a red giant, so that the Earth will be destroyed. However, this cannot happen for at least 5 billion years. The Sun will then shrink down to become a very small, very heavy star of the kind called a **white dwarf.** Finally, all its light and heat will leave it, and it will become cold and dead.

A larger and more massive star may blow up in what is called a **supernova** explosion. This leaves nothing behind except a patch of gas and a tiny, spinning, extremely dense object called a **pulsar.** And if a star is more massive still, it may even collapse until not even light can escape from it, and it will become a **black hole.** There are no nearby stars massive enough to explode as supernovae or turn themselves into black holes.

The Sun, though large to us, is regarded by astronomers as a dwarf star. In this picture the Sun is compared in size with six smaller dwarf stars, and with the planets Earth, Mars and Uranus. Kuiper's star (bottom right), though no bigger than Mars, has a mass equal to that of the Sun. It is so dense that a 'spoonful' of its material would weigh many metric tons if it were possible to bring it back to Earth.

The Dumb-bell Nebula. This is a planetary nebula, that is to say neither a planet nor a nebula. It is made up of a great cloud of gas which has been thrown out from a hot star near its center.

Nebulae and galaxies

A THOUSAND YEARS AGO, Arab astronomers noticed something very interesting close to the three bright stars which make up the Belt of Orion. It looked like a dim, misty patch. Later, when telescopes were invented, many other misty patches were found. They are known as **nebulae**; 'nebula' is the Latin word for 'cloud', 'nebulae' is the plural.

Binoculars will give a good view of the Orion Nebula, and with any small telescope the appearance is beautiful. The nebula is over 1000 light-years away. It is made up of gas, mainly hydrogen, and what we may call 'dust'. Stars are born inside nebulae of this kind, so that the Orion Nebula is a stellar nursery. Over 5 billion years ago, our Sun was born in a nebula of the same type.

In the year 1781 a French astronomer, Charles Messier, made a list of over a hundred objects which he described as nebulae. In fact, his list contains not only nebulae, but also star-clusters, which are collections of stars comparatively close together. The Seven Sisters or Pleiades cluster in the constellation of the Bull, not far from Orion, is one of these, and is easy to see with the naked eye. Messier also listed 'globular clusters', that is to say, clusters shaped like globes, all of which are very distant, and which lie around the edges of our Galaxy.

The Galaxy itself is a flattened system. We can compare its shape with that of two fried eggs stuck together back to back. The Sun is not near the center, but well out towards one edge. When we look along the main thickness of the system, we can see many stars in almost the same direction. It is this which causes the appearance of the Milky Way. The stars in the Milky Way are not really crowded together, and they are in no danger of bumping into each other.

William Herschel, discoverer of the planet Uranus, was the first man to give a fairly good picture of the shape of the Galaxy. He also turned his telescopes towards other objects

The Orion Nebula. This is a cloud made up of gas and dust. The nebula is over 1000 light-years away from us in space. It is given its beautiful color by the light of hot, young stars in the center of the nebula.

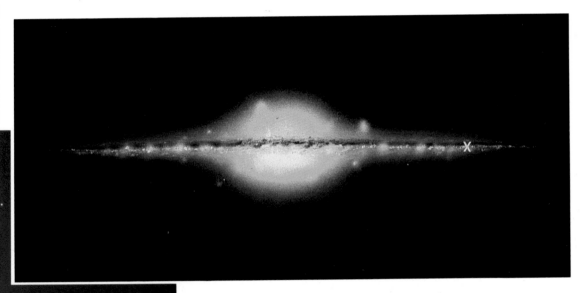

Our Galaxy as it would be seen, from the side. The Sun and our own planetary system, marked X, is away from the center. When we look up into the night sky and see the Milky Way, we are looking right through the center of the Galaxy to the far side. Our Galaxy is just one of millions of other galaxies.

Sir William Herschel (1738–1822)

which had been classed as nebulae, but which did not seem to be made up of gas in the same way as the Orion Nebula. Herschel made the bold suggestion that they might be separate star-systems or galaxies, well beyond the edge of our own Galaxy.

For many years it was impossible to decide whether or not this idea was correct. The final clue was given by stars which do not shine steadily, but brighten and fade regularly over periods of a few days. They do this because they are swelling and shrinking, changing in lumi-

The 2.5-m Hooker reflector at Mount Wilson, in southern California. Telescopes are often sited, as is this one, high up on mountains where the atmosphere is clear and good for viewing.

nosity or brightness as they do so. Some of these variable stars are particularly useful. The longer they take to brighten and fade, the more luminous they really are. This means that we can measure their real luminosity by observation, and we can then find out the stars' distances from the Earth.

In 1923 the American astronomer Edwin Hubble, using what was then the largest telescope in the world (the Mount Wilson 2.5-m reflector) found short-period variable stars in some of the starry nebulae. At once he saw that the systems were well beyond our system, and could only be separate galaxies. A few are visible with the naked eye, but most are much too faint. This is because their distances are so great. For example we know of galaxies at least 10 billion light-years away.

Many of the galaxies are spiral, like whirlpools; it has been found that our own Galaxy is a spiral, with the Sun close to the edge of one of the spiral arms. It has also been found that apart from a few of the closest systems, all the galaxies are moving away from us, so that the whole universe is expanding.

Modern telescopes can show at least a billion galaxies each made up of many millions of stars. We have certainly come a long way since mankind believed the Earth to be the most important body in the sky.

Radio waves from space

THROW A STONE into a calm pond, and you will set up ripples or waves. The distance between the top of one wave and the top of the next is called the **wavelength.** Light, too, is a wave motion, and the color of the light depends upon the wavelength. Red light has the longest wavelength, and then come orange, yellow, green, blue and violet. Yet even the wavelength of red light is very short and is only a tiny fraction of a millimeter.

Waves with wavelengths shorter than that of violet light do not affect our eyes, but can be measured in other ways. We have ultraviolet

(as used in sun lamps) and X-rays. If the wavelength is longer than that of red light, these are called radio waves. Bodies in the sky send out radiations at all wavelengths, from the very short to the very long.

Radio astronomy has become of great importance in modern science. It began in 1931, when an American radio engineer named Jansky realized that his equipment was picking up radio waves from the Milky Way. In the 1950s special radio telescopes were built. The most famous of them is at Jodrell Bank, in England. It collects the radio waves by using a

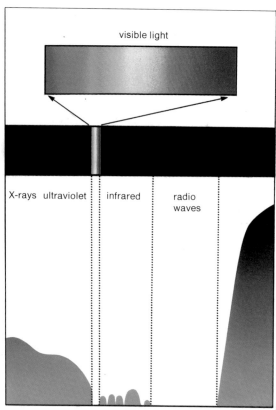

Electromagnetic waves spread out through space in every direction. Some of these waves, such as ultraviolet and X-rays, are absorbed by the Earth's atmosphere, so we are protected from them. The waves which pass through 'windows' in the atmosphere are visible light, some infrared waves, and radio waves. We use the latter in radio astronomy.

The 77-m radio telescope at Jodrell Bank, in England. The 'dish' focuses radio waves in much the same way as an ordinary telescope focuses light waves.

huge metal 'dish', 77 m in diameter. The radio waves are brought to focus, but no visible picture is produced. You cannot look through a radio telescope. Instead, the waves are recorded as a tracing on graph paper.

It was soon found that the Sun is a radio source, but other radio sources were found well outside the solar system. Using the Jodrell Bank radio telescope, Sir Bernard Lovell and his team found many such sources. Other radio telescopes were built in many countries – not all of them in the form of metal dishes, but all carrying out the same kind of work.

Radio sources are of many kinds. Some are old supernovae – that is to say, stars which have exploded. A famous case is that of the Crab Nebula, a patch of gas in the constellation of the Bull. It is all that remains of a supernova which blazed out in the year 1054 and became bright enough to be seen in broad daylight for a few weeks. Inside the Crab Nebula is a very small, quickly spinning pulsar. It spins round thirty times every second, sending out radio waves as it does so. Many other pulsars are also known to be the remains of supernovae.

Some galaxies, too, send out strong radio waves, and there are also strange objects called **quasars** which are smaller than ordinary galaxies but much more powerful. The first quasar was found in 1963. Hundreds are now known, but even today we are not sure of their nature. They may well be the centers of very active galaxies. The most distant quasar known is at least 13 billion light-years away.

Quasars, like most galaxies, are moving away from us at very great speeds – very near to the speed of light for the most distant quasar. The further away a quasar or a galaxy is, the faster it seems to be going. This may set a limit to the universe which we can study, because if an object is racing away at the speed of light we will be unable to see it.

We do not know exactly how the universe began. According to one idea it began with a big bang over 15 billion years ago. It started to expand, so that first galaxies, then stars and then planets were formed. Another theory suggests that the universe expands and contracts regularly, so that every 80 billion years or so there is a new big bang. But even if either of these ideas is correct, we still do not know much about the creation of the universe. This may even be a puzzle which we will never solve.

The 64-m radio telescope at Parkes, New South Wales, Australia. This, like the Jodrell Bank telescope, is fully steerable.

The Crab Nebula is 6000 light-years away from us. It is a source of radio waves, but apart from this sends out radiation at nearly all wavelengths. It contains a pulsar which flashes as it spins more than thirty times a second.

Satellites and spaceships

In the second century AD a Greek writer named Lucian told a story about a trip to the Moon. Of course, he did not mean to be taken seriously. He did not even know how far away the Moon is, but his story showed that the idea of space travel is certainly not new.

Much later, in 1865, the French author Jules Verne wrote a story in which his travellers were fired from the Earth to the Moon in a hollow globe, shot out of the barrel of a big gun. He was careful to give the correct speed – 11.2 km per second, which, as we have seen, is the Earth's escape velocity. However, no space-gun could ever work. Apart from the fact that the globe would be burned away by rubbing against the atmosphere, the shock of starting off at escape velocity would turn the unfortunate travellers into jelly.

Neither can we use aircraft to reach the Moon. This is because they cannot fly unless there is air around them, and there is not much air higher than a few kilometers above the Earth's surface. Most of the 380,000-km gap between the Earth and the Moon is airless space.

The key to the problem of space travel was found by a Russian named Tsiolkovskii, who wrote articles and books about it more than eighty years ago. He planned to use the power of the rocket. In an ordinary firework rocket, a hollow tube is filled with gunpowder. When the powder is lit, hot gas shoots out through the exhaust, and makes the rocket move. The rocket pushes against itself, so to speak, and does not need to have air around it.

Apollo 17 night launch. The Saturn V rocket sends the Apollo spacecraft on its way to the Moon, December 7, 1972. This was to be the last manned flight to the Moon before the start of the Skylab project.

View of Skylab from the Command and Service Module, June 1973, after repairs had been carried out.

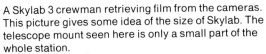

A Skylab 3 crewman retrieving film from the cameras. This picture gives some idea of the size of Skylab. The telescope mount seen here is only a small part of the whole station.

Artist's impression of the telecommunications satellite Intelsat IV. Here the nose cone shroud is shown at the moment of being jettisoned, since it is no longer needed.

In 1926 an American rocket engineer, Robert Goddard, built and tested the first rocket which used liquid fuels instead of solid gunpowder. During the Second World War powerful liquid-fuel rockets were built by the Germans to carry explosives. Later, when the war was over, the Americans started to build rockets of their own, not to carry explosives, but to launch artificial satellites.

In 1957 there came a major development. The Russians, who also had been testing rockets, successfully launched the first satellite, Sputnik 1. It was about the size of a football, and carried little apart from a radio transmitter, but it marked the beginning of the Space Age. It was taken up by a rocket and put into a path round the Earth. It then kept on moving in the same way as the real moon does because there was nothing to stop it. In fact it was not quite outside the top of the air layer, so that it was slowed down and finally burned away in the lower atmosphere in January 1958.

The first American satellite followed in the same year, and in 1961 came the first manned space flight, by the Russian cosmonaut Yuri Gagarin. Since then, thousands of satellites have been sent up, and many manned flights have been made. The first true space stations were launched in the 1970s. The American Skylab station carried three crews in succession, while in 1982 two Russians, Anatoly Berezovoy and Valentin Lebedev, set up a record by staying on board the space station Salyut 7 for 211 days.

Inside a spaceship orbiting the Earth there is no feeling of weight, so that if you hold out an object and release it the object will not drop. This is known as zero gravity. It does not seem to be dangerous, but it is certainly strange.

Artificial satellites may often be seen, looking like stars moving slowly across the sky. They have proved to be very useful. For example, they can give early warnings of dangerous storms developing out at sea, and they are used as radio and television stations. Furthermore, without artificial satellites, it would be difficult for a television station in, say, New York to transmit a program to, for example, London, England.

Jack Lousma testing the Astronaut Maneuvering Unit inside Skylab's workshop. Movement of this mini-spacecraft is controlled by gas jets.

27

Men on the Moon

In 1963, President Kennedy announced that America hoped to put a man on the Moon before 1970. At the time few people believed that this would be possible, but work went ahead quickly and before long the Apollo project was well under way.

One problem which spaceship planners have to face is that of fuel. No vehicle can carry enough fuel to take off from the Earth, fly to the Moon, land there, and take off again for the return journey. Neither can a rocket lift off from the Earth's surface too quickly; if it did, it would burn away. The only possibility is to use what is termed a **step-rocket** (something Tsiolkovskii had realized so long before).

A step-rocket is made up of several separate rockets, mounted one on top of the other. At the start of the journey, the large bottom 'step' does all the work, and lifts the vehicle high into the atmosphere. When it has used up all its fuel it breaks away and falls back to the ground. The second 'step' continues the journey by using its own engines, and extra 'steps' can be added if needed. It is a clumsy way of doing things, but at present there is nothing better.

While the Apollo spaceships were being made and tested, the Moon was studied from close range by unmanned vehicles. Some of these circled the Moon and mapped the surface while others landed there to make sure that the ground was firm enough to bear the weight of a spacecraft. The Russians, too, launched spacecraft of this sort, though as yet they have made no effort to send men to the Moon.

The Apollo program had its first triumph in July 1969 with No 11 in the series. The launching vehicle was as tall as the Capitol in Washington, D.C., and the three travellers, Neil Armstrong, Edwin Aldrin and Michael Collins, were in the very top part. The launching was carried out without any problems. The large lower step broke away, and the upper part was put into a path towards the Moon.

Apollo 11. One of the astronauts is seen erecting the solar wind sheet. This collects atomic particles from the Sun. It was rolled up before departure and carried back to Earth for examination by scientists.

Apollo 14. In this photograph, taken from the Moon's surface, the Earth is seen rising over the lunar horizon. When seen from space the Earth shows phases, just as the Moon does to us. In this picture the Earth is in its 'new' phase, in the shape of a crescent. At this time the Moon would appear nearly full when viewed from the Earth.

Apollo 14. Alan Shepard on the surface of the Moon, photographed through the window of the Lunar Module.

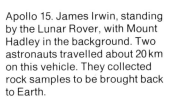

Apollo 15. James Irwin, standing by the Lunar Rover, with Mount Hadley in the background. Two astronauts travelled about 20 km on this vehicle. They collected rock samples to be brought back to Earth.

(left) Apollo 17. Jack Schmitt, the first geologist to go to the Moon, is seen collecting rock samples with the lunar rake.

Apollo 17. After spending 75 hours on the Moon's surface Cernan and Schmitt approach the Command Module for the final link-up.

When Apollo 11 came close to the Moon, it was put into a closed path round it. Then Armstrong and Aldrin went into a smaller vehicle, the 'lunar **module**', (named *Eagle*), which had been brought for the actual landing. Leaving Collins behind in the rest of the spacecraft, Armstrong and Aldrin used the motors of the module to take them down. They hovered close above the lunar surface, and then listeners all over the world heard Armstrong's voice: 'The *Eagle* has landed'.

Armstrong and Aldrin found themselves in a strange world. The sky was black even in the daytime. They had only one-sixth of their Earth weight, and when they went outside the spaceship they had to wear special suits because of the lack of air. When they had finished their work, they lifted off again and rejoined Collins for the return journey. Only the top part of the original Apollo 11, a 7-m cone, survived to splash down safely in the sea.

Since then there have been six more trips to the Moon, of which only one (Apollo 13) was unsuccessful. The Apollo program ended in 1972.

Since 1972 no more travellers have been to the Moon but we know that it can be done, and within the next few tens of years it will even be possible to set up a proper lunar base. When this is done, it will be of the greatest value to all mankind.

The planets – and beyond

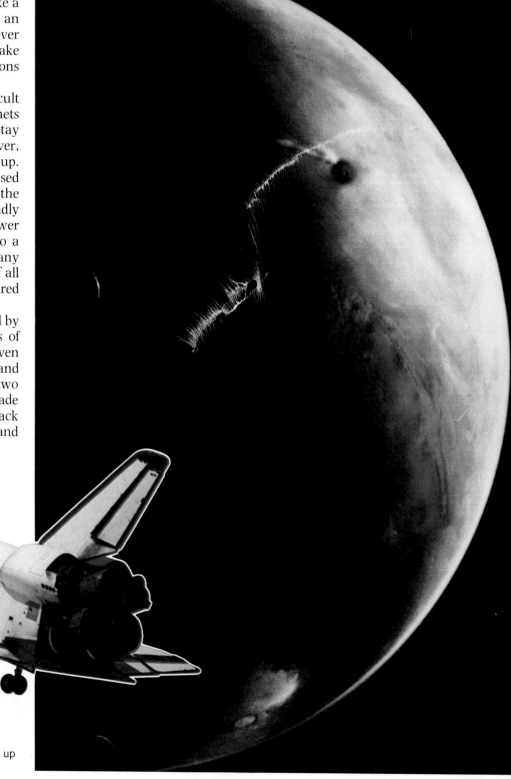

SPACE RESEARCH has made quick progress. The United States has developed the Space Shuttle which takes off like a rocket, flies like a spaceship and lands like a glider. Unlike an ordinary rocket it can be used over and over again. This means that it will be able to take men and supplies to and from the space stations which are planned for the near future.

Reaching the planets is much more difficult than reaching the Moon because the planets are so much further away, and they do not stay close to the Earth, as the Moon does. However, many unmanned probes have been sent up. The first was Mariner 2, in 1962, which passed within 34,000 km of Venus and sent back the first close-range news from that unfriendly world. Mariner was launched by rocket power and put into a path which swung it in to a meeting with Venus. The journey took many weeks even though Venus is the nearest of all the planets. At its closest it is only a hundred times as far away as the Moon.

Another Mariner, No 10, has also passed by Mercury, and sent back to Earth pictures of the mountains and craters there. Mars is even more interesting and both Americans and Russians have sent spacecraft to it. The two Vikings, launched by the United States, made gentle landings there in 1976, sending back pictures direct from the surface. Jupiter and

The Space Shuttle, Columbia, glides in to land. The reusable craft is enabling giant leaps forward in space research.

Mars as photographed by Viking 2 at a distance of 419,000 km. Clearly visible is the giant volcano Ascraeus Mons, with its white clouds of ice showing up well against the planet's red color.

A view of the famous canyons on Mars. Color images such as this were formed by a complex, computer-aided system on board the Viking spacecraft. Here you can see how several pictures have been taken, using color filters, from slightly different angles. To produce the end result, the computer has had to change each image slightly in order to avoid a blur.

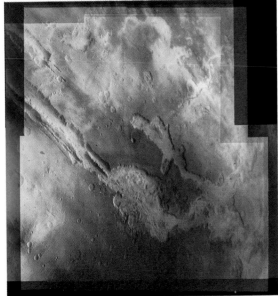

The Great Red Spot of Jupiter from Voyager 1. Thought to be a gigantic whirling storm, it has a surface area greater than that of the Earth. The reason for its color remains a mystery.

Saturn have also been bypassed. The best results came from Voyagers 1 and 2, both of which went by Jupiter and then on to Saturn. They sent back clear pictures of Jupiter's clouds and moons and the wonderful rings of Saturn. Voyager 2 is now on its way to the next planet, Uranus, which should be bypassed in January 1986. Neither of the Voyagers will ever come back. They will escape from the solar system, and when we lose radio contact with them they will be lost to us for ever.

It takes years for a spaceship to reach the outer planets. To reach the nearest star would take a rocket thousands of years, and there is no hope of our being able to do this, at least for the present. Yet even with the stars, space research can be of great help. Once above the atmosphere, there is nothing to blot out the **radiation** coming from space. A large space telescope, circling the Earth and controlled from the ground, might be able to show planets moving round some of the closer stars. Uninterrupted by Earth's atmosphere it will outperform all ground-based telescopes.

One particularly interesting question is: can there be life on worlds away from the Earth? The planets in our solar system do not seem to be suitable and even Mars has shown no sign of life. However, since the Sun is an ordinary star, it is sensible to believe that the Earth is an ordinary planet. Other planets, moving round other suns, may well support life, and there may well be civilizations much more advanced than ours.

Whether we can ever get in touch with other civilizations is something we do not yet know. But at least we have learned more during the past hundred years than we had been able to do in the previous thousand years. Astronomy is a fast moving science and new discoveries are being made all the time. The story of astronomy is not over. Indeed, it may be only just beginning.

Some two weeks after the start of its journey in 1977, Voyager 1 took this picture of the Earth and its companion the Moon. It had already travelled 11.5 million km. To reach the outer planets of our solar system, the craft's journey is to take several years, covering distances which to us are difficult to comprehend.

An artist's impression of the Space Telescope orbiting the Earth at a height of 500 km. It will have clear views of distant stars and galaxies.

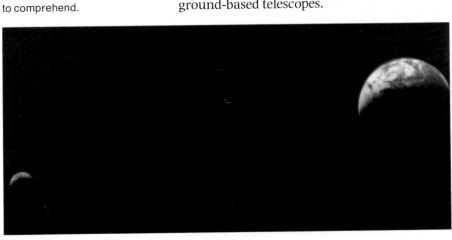

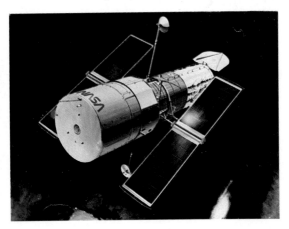

Living and working in space

THE IDEA of sending humans into space is a very old one, but only fairly recently has it become possible to do this. Originally it was thought that the human body would be unable to adapt to conditions in space. The main problems, it was thought, would be those of zero gravity, cosmic radiation and bombardment by meteorites.

When a spacecraft is moving round the Earth in what is termed free fall, the crew members have no sensation of weight. One way to understand this is to imagine a coin placed upon a book and both being allowed to fall. Before the book is dropped the coin is pressing down upon it. In relation to the book the coin is 'heavy'. During descent, the book is falling away from under the coin. The coin is no longer pressing and in relation to the book it has become weightless. The same applies to an astronaut inside a spacecraft in orbit. The two are moving in the same direction at the same rate.

Weightlessness is a strange sensation. In this situation an object held out at arm's length and then released will not fall. Weightless liquid will not pour, and objects, unless fixed to something are apt to float about inside the spacecraft. Despite this, zero gravity conditions are not harmful, even over periods of several months, as the Russian experiments have shown. It is not so certain that they will also be harmless over much longer periods, as would be involved in a journey to Mars or Venus.

This photograph of the cargo bay of space shuttle Columbia *(opposite)* was taken by a member of the crew from inside the shuttle cabin. In the fore-ground is a pallet of experiments. This was Columbia's second trip and it lasted for 54 hours.

This Landsat photograph shows ice coverage in the far north of Canada. Pictures like this one help ships to find their way through the ice fields which are always changing.

Cosmic radiation has not so far proved a real hazard. There have been no problems with small, solid bodies such as meteorites.

Working in space may be unfamiliar, but it has various advantages. Since materials in space have no weight, some scientific processes can be carried out which would be impossible on Earth. In this environment it is possible to produce perfect crystals and special strong metals which are very pure. Medical research is also of great importance since conditions of zero gravity cannot be properly simulated upon Earth.

By using weather satellites, a constant watch can be kept upon the Earth's atmosphere. These are used to study large scale movements of air masses, and whole weather systems. As a result the world now has advance warning of dangerous storms and hurricanes developing far out to sea. Since 1966, the entire globe has been covered daily by weather satellites and thousands of lives have been saved. People living in threatened areas have had ample time to move out of danger.

A satellite system known as 'Landsat' is used to collect information about the Earth that is impossible to gather in any other way. Landsat uses a process called **remote sensing** in which

Skylab. Joseph Kerwin, a doctor of medicine, gives his commander, Charles Conrad, an oral examination. Even the paper for Kerwin's notes is floating, weightless, near at hand.

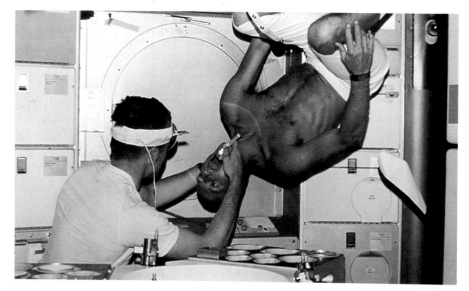

the Earth is scanned to reveal different patterns of radiation. Computer centers on the ground translate the information received from Landsat into photographs. The photographs use false color, and these different colors show variations in radiation. Scientists are then able to detect such things as areas which may be rich in oil and diseased areas of tropical forests. It is also much easier to trace water pollution, and to track oil slicks far out at sea.

The environment of space is ideal as an astronomical observatory. In 1985, the Space Shuttle will be used to launch the 12-metric-ton space telescope, a 2.4-m reflector. Because there is no atmosphere in space to distort the image, the telescope will be able to detect objects fifty times fainter than can be seen now.

The Space Shuttle can be thought of as a large truck. Although expensive to launch, the shuttle can be used over and over again and during the 1980s many shuttle flights will take place. This means that more and more research in space will be carried out, and whole laboratories will be taken up there.

All the astronauts who have spent prolonged periods in space state that conditions are by no means uncomfortable. The main problem is in readjusting to the normal sensation of weight upon return to Earth. It may be more difficult after flights lasting for very long periods. At least there are grounds for believing that the risks are not so great as used to be thought before the pioneer flight of Yuri Gagarin in April 1961.

The first American female astronaut, Sally Ride, conducting experiments on Space Shuttle mission STS-6.

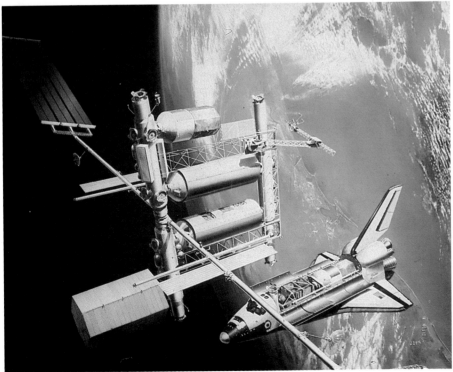

An orbiting space station of the future *(left)* with shuttle supply ship alongside. Note the solar energy panel. Space stations similar to this should be in service by the year 2000.

Inner space

IT WILL BE CLEAR from the first part of this book that astronomers are concerned with a universe so huge as to be unimaginable. The objects in space are separated by very great distances. Even light may take many millions of years to cover the distance between them. Physicists, on the other hand, are learning about a world which is incredibly tiny.

We live in a universe of immense variety. Our world is only one of many planets, but it is full of **matter.** We use this word matter to describe anything that occupies space, even including the air we breathe but cannot see. All matter, including the air we breathe, is made up of smaller and smaller parts.

In the rest of this book we will be looking at the smallest and most basic building bricks of the universe. They are the **atoms**, from which we believe all matter in the universe is made. It seems likely that the great range of objects, such as white dwarfs, black holes and quasars, may all be made up of similar types of atomic **particles**, the tiny pieces of matter which scientists have detected in laboratories here on Earth.

Scientists have a special language which they use when describing atoms. We will be using some of this language in the rest of this book. When talking about atoms we have to use very large and very small numbers. Rather than use very long numbers, which take up a lot

of space on the paper, we use a special code, called powers of ten or indices. You can refer to this code in the panel alongside.

When scientists describe objects in the universe, both large and small, they do not talk about weight. Instead, they refer to an object's **mass**, which is measured in kilograms.

The great physicist Isaac Newton said that the mass of an object was a measure of the amount of matter contained within it. Unlike weight, the mass of an object does not change because of the force of gravity. Clearly, an elephant has a very large mass, far greater than a mouse. But an elephant weighed on the Moon would be lighter than when weighed on Earth because the Moon's gravity is less than the gravity of Earth. However, its mass would remain the same.

To give you an idea of how small an atom is, try this experiment next time you go to the movies. Look up at the beam of light passing from the projector to the screen. Inside this beam you will see the glint of thousands of tiny dust particles floating to and fro in the air. Each of these dust particles is more than 50,000 atoms across. It is little wonder that we cannot see these atoms and they are so numerous that they can never be counted. Although these atoms are very small, scientists have found that they are made up of even smaller particles.

Number shorthand

We often need to use very large and very small numbers in science. It is sometimes easier and certainly saves space to use a code called 'powers of ten'. This system is used by scientists to describe something very large, such as the distance of the Sun from the Earth, or something very small such as the size of the atom. The system works like this:

$$1000 = 1 \times 10 \times 10 \times 10 = 1 \times 10^3$$
$$100 = 1 \times 10 \times 10 \qquad = 1 \times 10^2$$
$$10 = 1 \times 10 \qquad = 1 \times 10^1$$
$$1 = 1 \times 1 \qquad = 1 \times 10^0$$
$$0.1 \quad \text{or } 1/10 \qquad = 1 \times 10^{-1}$$
$$0.01 \quad \text{or } 1/100 \qquad = 1 \times 10^{-2}$$
$$0.001 \quad \text{or } 1/1000 \qquad = 1 \times 10^{-3}$$

The distance of the Sun from the Earth is given below in different units of measurement:

Distance is
150,000,000 km or 1.5×10^8 km
or in meters
D = 150,000,000,000 or 1.5×10^{11} m
or in millimeters
D = 150,000,000,000,000
or 1.5×10^{14} mm

As you can see, the code begins to save space once the numbers become very large indeed.

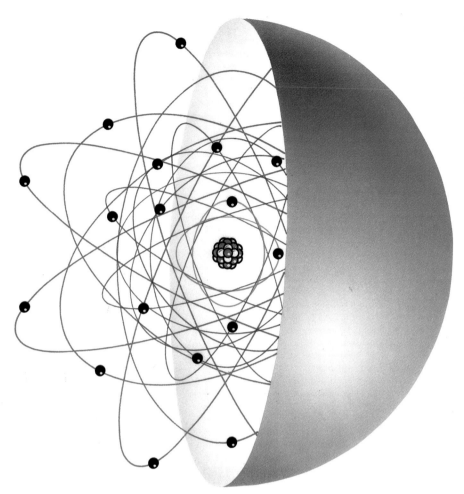

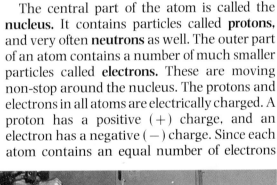

All human beings like to measure things as a way of understanding them. In thinking of Outer Space and Inner Space we cannot avoid comparing sizes. This is not easy because Outer Space is so vast that we cannot begin to think about the sizes and distances. We can at least look up into the sky and realize that there are huge expanses of emptiness. However, we cannot do this with Inner Space, inside matter itself, because atoms are so small. In fact, an atom is as 'empty' as the solar system. The nucleus of an atom is as small in comparison to the whole atom as the Sun is compared with the orbits of the planets. Put another way, matter itself is very empty.

In a single atom *(left)* the electrons are seen orbiting around the nucleus in paths not unlike those of the planets around the Sun.

Skylab 4. Gerald Carr poses as a strong man by holding Ed Gibson up with one finger. In zero gravity Gibson would in fact float there without even the finger to support him. Gibson has the same 'mass' in space as he does on Earth; only his 'weight' changes.

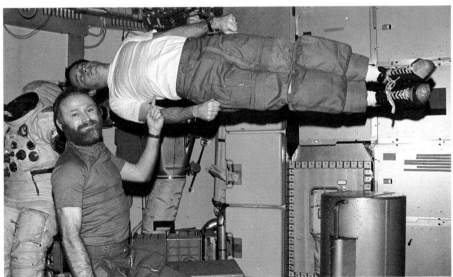

The central part of the atom is called the **nucleus.** It contains particles called **protons,** and very often **neutrons** as well. The outer part of an atom contains a number of much smaller particles called **electrons.** These are moving non-stop around the nucleus. The protons and electrons in all atoms are electrically charged. A proton has a positive $(+)$ charge, and an electron has a negative $(-)$ charge. Since each atom contains an equal number of electrons and protons, these cancel each other out so that matter as a whole has no electrical charge. A neutron has a mass almost the same as the proton, but it carries no charge.

Before 1930, scientists thought that atoms were made up of only three different particles, protons, neutrons and electrons. However, in recent years scientists have discovered that there are many other particles inside the atom, which are quite different from these three. Many of these new particles only exist for a tiny fraction of a second before **decaying** or changing into other different particles. Over one hundred of these **sub-atomic** particles have been detected and the number is steadily growing as research continues.

Could these many particles be made up of just a few even tinier ones? Scientists now think this is so. They believe that most particles, including the proton and the neutron, can be made up by combinations of just four different particles called **quarks.** Possibly as many as six quarks exist. However, the electron is an exception. It is one of a small family of particles called **leptons.** These are not made up of quarks, and they remain alone. They do not join together to form other particles. Perhaps the universe consists of just two types of particles: quarks and leptons.

The beginnings of scientific discovery

ANYTHING THAT HELPS us to understand things can be called a discovery. Progress in early science nearly always happened by chance discovery. We might call these 'accidental experiments'. It is likely that one of the earliest scientific accidents was the production of copper from an ore. Some charcoal in a hot fire, mixing with the ore, would make copper. Lumps of copper would be found when the fire cooled down. We will never know if this was the way copper was first made, because very little was written down about science until the sixteenth century.

What we know about early scientists has been gathered together from small pieces of information. Carvings on stone, wood and metal objects sometimes show the skills of craftsmen. They tell us that there were Egyptians and Babylonians making objects in gold, silver, copper and lead thousands of years ago. The Assyrians were making colored glass in 700 BC.

The discovery of the tomb of Tutankhamen has shown us some of the wonderful skills of the Egyptian craftsmen. The gold coffin that surrounded the mummy of the king weighed over one metric ton and had been shaped to look like the mummy. Inside was the famous death mask, also of beaten gold and inlaid with precious stones and glass. The tomb also contained objects made of cotton which had been dyed and woven into patterns. Dyeing is one more example of early chemistry. One or two iron objects were in the tomb as well, and this shows that the Egyptians were improving their skills at finding and using new metals. It is much harder to make iron from its ore than it is to make copper.

Perhaps the word 'chemistry' itself comes from the ancient name for Egypt, Chem, the dark land. Certainly, the word **alchemist** came from the ancient Greek and was used to describe the early scientists.

The Egyptians and their neighbors were great technicians – they were skilled at making and doing things. The Greeks produced the first **philosophers.** These men were thinkers who tried to make sense of what they saw in the world about them. One of these was Aristotle who lived in Greece about 350 BC. He thought that all things in the world were made up of just

This wall painting from an Egyptian tomb, 1380 BC, shows goldsmiths and craftsmen with their working tools. The Egyptians were very skilled in various arts based on metals, glass, plant oils and dyeing. Egypt is often looked upon as the birthplace of chemistry.

36

The death mask *(left)* of King Tutankhamen, who reigned in ancient Egypt about 1600BC. The solid gold coffin weighed more than 100 kg. The discovery of his tomb, almost untouched, in 1922, caused a great stir. The Egyptians knew how to beat and shape gold, and they were superb sculptors.

A 17th century laboratory in Amsterdam, with the chemist at work. At that time scientists had few chemicals and poor equipment. They worked with substances such as mercury, sulfur and salt. They also helped the doctors of the day with medicines made largely from plants and herbs. Perhaps their greatest interest of all was doing experiments with combustion (burning), since fire itself was still an unexplained mystery.

four **elements**, which he called earth, air, fire and water. He said that if the amounts of each element when mixed together were changed, a different substance was produced. This started the idea that it was possible to change one substance into another and the search began for something that would change common metals into gold. This mystery substance became known as the **Philosopher's Stone.**

Meanwhile, in China, alchemists had been searching for a different sort of Philosopher's Stone. This was a substance which would help people to live for much longer periods of time.

It is not easy to work out what the alchemists did, since much of their work was written down in a sort of code. However, they did help modern science by inventing ways of separating substances and making them pure. These processes, called **distilling** and **subliming**, were both used by alchemists and we still find old pictures of these methods being used.

Techniques like these were also used by skilled craftsmen – glassmakers, **pharmacists** who made drugs and medicines, and **metallurgists** whose work was to do with metals. The knowledge was handed on by word of mouth. In the sixteenth and seventeenth centuries books were written which collected this information together, and they give us the first real idea of how skilful these craftsmen had become.

As the methods of the alchemists and the craftsmen became better known they were used more widely. Paracelsus used them to find ways of healing the sick, and he was the first person to gather together the chemical knowledge of the sixteenth century.

Chemists of these times had to use the few chemicals which were available to them. They had minerals and ores which were found naturally, and some pure substances such as sulfur, mercury and carbon. Paracelsus used sulfur, mercury and salt a great deal, and many other chemists followed him.

In Arabia, a Persian called Abu Ali Ibn Sina (known to the Europeans as Avicenna) had also worked on cures for illnesses, and he wrote two books about them. He also wrote on other subjects and he was one of the first to doubt the recipes of the alchemists for making one metal into another. It was several hundred years later that scientists in Europe started to use Avicenna's idea in the study of chemistry, and to back them up with carefully controlled scientific experiments.

The Age of Reason

CHEMISTRY really started to develop as a science about three hundred years ago. In those days there were no specially trained chemists as there are today. The ideas came from men who had other occupations. Joseph Priestley was a pastor, and a teacher of languages and literature. Robert Boyle was the fourteenth child of the Earl of Cork. He started studying chemistry after nearly being accidently poisoned. Antoine Lavoisier came from a rich French family and was a brilliant lawyer.

Each one of these men developed new theories about chemistry. Boyle did not like the ideas of Aristotle and Paracelsus, and he wrote a book called *The Sceptical Chemist*. In it he said that nobody had proved any of the old ideas by experiments. He also offered his own definition of an **element.** Boyle said that the mistake Aristotle and Paracelsus had made was to say that there were only a few elements, and some mixture of these would make all other substances.

Nobody had questioned this idea until Robert Boyle, but he himself did not offer any proof of his own definition of an element. His definition was that, if you could not break up one substance into others, it should be thought of as an element. Nobody really argued with his theory, and it may be that he did not take the idea further because he did not have to defend it.

The Sceptical Chemist was published in 1661, and shortly afterwards another idea was put

Joseph Priestley, 1733–1804. His discovery of oxygen in 1774 helped other scientists to an understanding of gases and how they behave.

Robert Boyle, 1627–91, was a philosopher and scientist who attacked the old theories of the alchemists.

Antoine Lavoisier, 1743–94, the French scientist who founded modern chemistry. He gave oxygen its name.

forward to explain what happens when things burn. Chemists have always been fascinated by changes in a substance when it is heated, and fire really had been the driving force behind all chemical ideas up to this point.

To explain what was seen when certain metals were heated, some scientists put forward the 'Phlogiston' theory. Phlogiston was supposed to be a substance which was driven out of a chemical when it was heated. Lead shrivels up and forms a yellow powder when it is strongly heated, and this powder was called a 'calx'. The idea was that calx plus phlogiston equals metal. The fact that lead gains weight when it is heated in air was not explained.

Several people supported this theory, including Joseph Priestley. He did a lot of experiments, but often made the results fit the phlogiston theory, instead of using them to produce a more logical idea. In 1774 he was heating things to see what sort of gas was produced. By chance he heated some 'mercury calx' (mercury oxide) and was astonished to see mercury being formed. At the same time a colorless gas was produced, which allowed a candle to burn with a brilliant flame.

He had discovered **oxygen**, one of the gases of the air. He explained this surprising result by saying that the new gas was air that had lost its phlogiston.

Priestley went to Paris, and met Lavoisier at a dinner party. He mentioned his discovery, and how he had prepared the gas. This chance meeting was to have a great influence on the way ideas in chemistry developed.

Priestley had to leave England after he had made some remarks which upset a lot of people. His house was burned down and his books destroyed. He came to America, where he died in 1804.

Lavoisier was in some ways the opposite of Priestley. He was a brilliant man, but also very observant and careful in drawing conclusions from his experiments. If the results of an experiment did not fit with an existing theory, he would try to change the theory. He destroyed the Phlogiston theory with a series of experiments. He showed that, if you seal a metal in a glass flask, and then heat it, the metal forms a powder, and some of the air in the flask is used up. Also, there is no change in the weight of the flask after the experiment. He thought that air must be made up of two gases, one of which combined with the metal when they were heated together.

It was shortly after carrying out these experiments that Lavoisier met Priestley and realized the true meaning of Priestley's experiment. He repeated Priestley's work, and then improved on it by heating mercury in air. When he did

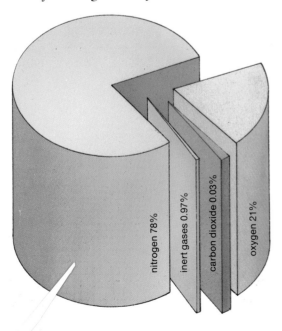

The oxygen in air is necessary for burning. In the picture above, the candle is burning in pure oxygen. It burns with a brilliant flame. When the oxygen is used up, the flame will die down and go out altogether. If a house catches fire, one of the rules is to close the doors and windows. This cuts down the oxygen supply and helps to keep the fire under control.

Air is not, as the alchemists thought, one of the elements. It is a mixture of gases. Oxygen is one-fifth of this mixture.

nitrogen 78%
inert gases 0.97%
carbon dioxide 0.03%
oxygen 21%

this he found that roughly one-sixth of the air was absorbed, and a red powder was formed on the surface of the mercury. Afterwards, when the red powder was heated, mercury and oxygen were formed again. He had discovered a number of things about **combustion**. He discovered that oxygen is a gas found in the air and that it combines with other substances.

Lavoisier used the name 'oxygen' after he found that sulfur, phosphorus, and carbon all burned in the gas to form acid substances. The word *oxygen* is based on Greek, and means 'acid maker'.

Lavoisier died, sadly, during the French Revolution. He was executed after being found guilty of adding water and other ingredients to tobacco. This was thought to be harmful to one's health.

The elements

AT THE END of the eighteenth century there was a great burst of activity in the world of chemistry. There were several reasons for this. One was the discovery by the Italian scientist Alessandro Volta of a way of making electricity. Electricity can be used to release metals from substances which contain them. Sir Humphry Davy discovered sodium and potassium in 1807, and many other metals could not have been found without the use of Volta's battery. The discovery of new elements was increasing rapidly, and scientists started looking for some kind of pattern. Could the new elements they were discovering be grouped together in some way?

John Dalton, 1766–1844. He is famous for the atomic theory and for creating a table of atomic weights of some of the elements.

In 1803, a quiet, gentle schoolmaster called John Dalton suggested that substances were made up of tiny particles called atoms, a word the Greeks had used over two thousand years before. He believed that each element had its own kind of atom, and that it would be possible to compare the weights of the different atoms. Dalton also invented some special signs for each of the elements known at that time. When these elements joined together he called the new substance a **compound** atom.

This was a new idea at that time. It was to become the starting point of modern theories of chemistry. Dalton's ideas were supported by many of the greatest chemists of the day. The Swedish scientist Baron Jons Jakob Berzelius added practical measurements to support Dalton's theories. This was a stroke of good luck for Dalton, as he was not brilliant when it came to experimental work. For instance, some of his work on gases was carried out using empty ink bottles as apparatus.

The weights of atoms of different elements were measured quite accurately. These 'weights' were not measured in grams or other units because the atoms were far too small. The weight of an atom was compared with that of other atoms, and the lightest of all was hydrogen. Dalton gave hydrogen a weight of 1, and called this its **atomic weight.**

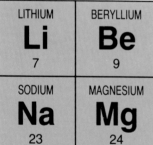

Magnesium (left), discovered in 1775, is the eighth most common element. It burns with a very bright light and is used in flares, flashbulbs and fireworks.

Iron (right), is a metal found in ores (rocks). It is smelted to make the pure metal. Most of it is used to make steel.

HYDROGEN **H** 1								
LITHIUM **Li** 7	BERYLLIUM **Be** 9							
SODIUM **Na** 23	MAGNESIUM **Mg** 24							
POTASSIUM **K** 39	CALCIUM **Ca** 40	SCANDIUM **Sc** 45	TITANIUM **Ti** 48	VANADIUM **V** 51	CHROMIUM **Cr** 52	MANGANESE **Mn** 55	IRON **Fe** 56	COBALT **Co** 59
RUBIDIUM **Rb** 85	STRONTIUM **Sr** 88	YTTRIUM **Y** 89	ZIRCONIUM **Zr** 91	NIOBIUM **Nb** 93	MOLYBDENUM **Mo** 96	TECHNETIUM **Tc** 98	RUTHENIUM **Ru** 101	RHODIUM **Rh** 103
CAESIUM **Cs** 133	BARIUM **Ba** 137	LANTHANUM **La** 139	HAFNIUM **Hf** 178	TANTALUM **Ta** 181	TUNGSTEN **W** 184	RHENIUM **Re** 186	OSMIUM **Os** 190	IRIDIUM **Ir** 192
FRANCIUM **Fr** 223	RADIUM **Ra** 226	ACTINIUM **Ac** 227						

This is a simplified version of the Periodic Table, showing 72 elements. It does not include a further 30 elements (known as the lanthanides and actinides). The elements arranged across the table are called 'periods'.

Those arranged vertically are known as 'groups'. There is a scientific connection either way. Each box shown in the table gives the name of the element, its symbol, and its atomic weight to the nearest whole number.

When several atomic weights had been worked out a pattern began to appear. The true pattern was not completely shown until nearly sixty years later. Several scientists had noticed that some elements, such as chlorine, bromine and iodine, were alike. It seemed that some of these elements were in 'family' groups, with members of the same family making similar chemicals when they reacted together.

Eventually, after a lot of work by many people, a Russian scientist, Dmitri Mendeleev, produced an arrangement of the elements, using the atomic weights as the pattern maker. He arranged all the known elements in groups of eight, and found that they formed 'families'. Perhaps his most important idea was that he was able to leave spaces in his table for elements that had not yet been discovered.

Mendeleev upset some of the best chemists with his ideas, because their work was shown to be inaccurate. However, his table of the elements was so logical that it was quickly accepted. Because of it, scientists worked hard to find the 'missing' elements. He had been able to make up his **Periodic Table** of the elements, as it was called, because of the work of many scientists before him. There was no sudden, brilliant discovery. Scientists from many countries had given a small part of the final result. Mendeleev had fitted the pieces together, like solving a jigsaw puzzle.

The modern form of Mendeleev's table shows us that elements can be arranged in groups. Each group contains chemicals which are alike in certain ways. If we take a group of metals as an example, we can see the 'family likeness'. Sodium and potassium have been known for nearly two hundred years, and lithium nearly as long. Two other metals, rubidium and caesium were discovered just before Mendeleev published his work in 1869. They are all soft, light metals, unlike iron and copper, and are never found as free metals. They react violently with water and other chemicals, forming substances which are very similar to each other.

Another group of elements is called the halogens. Of these, chlorine, bromine and iodine are the best known. Fluorine, discovered in 1886, is the other halogen. These are some of the most reactive elements known, and they attack most metals, forming similar products. One surprising thing is that two very reactive and dangerous elements, the metal sodium and the gas chlorine, form common salt when they react together.

Dmitri Mendeleev, 1834–1907. He was a Russian scientist who worked out the Periodic Table of elements. Only 63 elements were known at the time of his work. However, he was able to predict several other elements not discovered at that time. He left spaces for them in his table.

Neon (above), is an inert gas used in neon lighting. The element carbon occurs as diamonds, charcoal and graphite (left).

						HELIUM He 4
	BORON B 11	CARBON C 12	NITROGEN N 14	OXYGEN O 16	FLUORINE F 19	NEON Ne 20
	ALUMINUM Al 27	SILICON Si 28	PHOSPHORUS P 31	SULFUR S 32	CHLORINE Cl 35.5	ARGON Ar 40
NICKEL Ni 59	COPPER Cu 64	ZINC Zn 65	GALLIUM Ga 70	GERMANIUM Ge 73	ARSENIC As 75	SELENIUM Se 79	BROMINE Br 80	KRYPTON Kr 84
PALLADIUM Pd 106	SILVER Ag 108	CADMIUM Cd 112	INDIUM In 115	TIN Sn 119	ANTIMONY Sb 122	TELLURIUM Te 128	IODINE I 127	XENON Xe 131
PLATINUM Pt 195	GOLD Au 197	MERCURY Hg 201	THALLIUM Tl 204	LEAD Pb 207	BISMUTH Bi 209	POLONIUM Po 209	ASTATINE At 210	RADON Rn 222

KEY

HYDROGEN | ALKALI AND ALKALINE EARTH METALS | METALS | NON-METALS INCLUDING HALOGENS | NOBLE GASES

Elements, compounds and mixtures

SCIENTISTS in the past used the word 'element' in several different ways, but chemists now use the word very carefully. Any chemical we happen to choose is made up of several atoms joined together. If the atoms that make up one piece of the chemical are different, then the substance is called a **compound**. If the atoms are all the same the substance is an element.

To understand the difference between an element and a compound, let us look at the way water can be made from its elements:

Hydrogen + Oxygen → Water
The sign → means 'forms'

Sodium is a strange metal. It can be sliced with a knife to show a shiny, metallic surface. This quickly reacts with air to lose its shine. For this reason it is kept in a bottle of oil in the laboratory. The experiment *(above)* shows how sodium and the gas chlorine (two elements) combine to form salt (a compound). A lump of sodium is heated and then lowered into a gas jar containing chlorine. There is a flash of light and a chemical reaction takes place. The powder that is left is salt.

Hydrogen and oxygen are both elements and each one is made up of just one type of atom. When they join together, a lot of heat and a flash of light are given out. Sometimes an explosion takes place. The compound water is formed when two hydrogen atoms and one oxygen atom combine, or join together.

Compounds are often completely different from the elements that make them up. Water is a liquid, and it boils at 100°C. Oxygen and hydrogen are both gases, and to turn them into liquids the temperature has to be lowered by over 200°C.

An even more surprising change is seen when sodium and chlorine combine. Sodium is a metal with a silvery color, and chlorine is a green gas. Both these elements are dangerous, and chlorine was used as a poison gas in World War I. If some hot sodium is lowered into a jar of chlorine, there is a flash of light, and the jar fills with white smoke. The smoke gradually settles on the sides and bottom of the jar, and can be

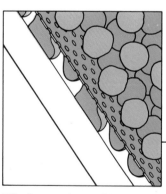

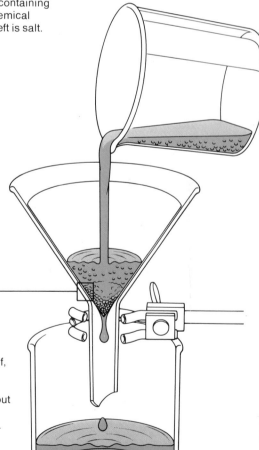

Filtration can be used to separate two substances from each other in a mixture. If, for example, grains of sand and salt are mixed together, we can separate them by filtration. Sand will not dissolve in water, but salt will. Water is added to the mixture which is then poured through a filter into a container. The sand is left behind. If the liquid is then heated *(right)*, the water will evaporate, leaving the salt behind as a powder.

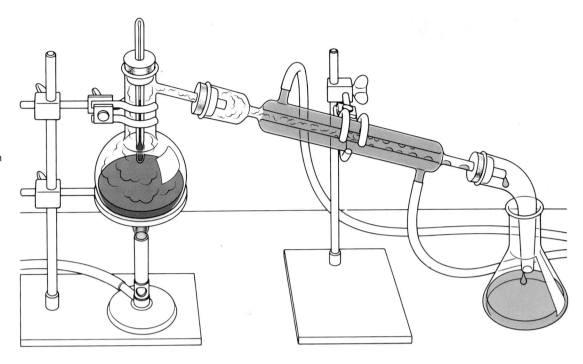

Distillation can be used to separate mixtures of liquids with different boiling points from each other. The boiling point of water is 100°C, that of, for example, alcohol is 78°C. In the picture a mixture of dirty water and alcohol is being separated. The mixture would be heated to the boiling point of alcohol. The alcohol is given off as a vapor. As it cools in the condenser it returns to its liquid state. The dirty water is left behind in the flask.

scraped up. It is a fine white powder, and quite harmless – it is common salt.

Common salt is, then, a compound made from sodium and chlorine. Its chemical name is sodium chloride. To get the sodium and chlorine back again is difficult, because they are firmly joined together. The compound has to be split up using a battery, and it is not possible to separate these elements easily in any other way. Compounds, once they are made, have to be forced apart if you want to recover the elements that are in them.

Many substances can be mixed together without any reaction taking place – they do not combine. A **mixture** of this type can be separated into the different substances much more easily. Chemists use a number of methods to separate substances, and some of these methods were developed by the alchemists many years ago. Two of the most common methods used for separating substances are **filtration** and **distillation**.

Filtration can be used to separate two substances if one of them dissolves in water and the other one does not. An example of this sort of mixture is salt and sand. Salt dissolves in water, forming a liquid, while sand does not change. If the mixture of the liquid and the sand is poured into a filter, the liquid runs through while the sand is held back. A filter is only a barrier with small holes in it; something small enough will pass through the holes. As liquids are made up of very small particles, they will pass through filters, while most solid substances will not.

You can get the salt back from the liquid by heating it gently, so that the water turns into steam. Salt is left behind as a white powder.

Sometimes two different liquids have to be separated, and the method known as distillation is used. When liquids are heated, they will boil, and when this happens they turn into a gas. If one liquid boils more easily than the other one, it can be turned into a gas, leaving the other liquid behind. Once this is done, the gas can be cooled down, and it will **condense**, or turn back into a liquid. This process is called distillation, and it is used by the oil industry. Oil is a mixture of substances and most of these can be separated by distilling them. The products include gasoline, diesel fuel and fuel oil.

How can a mixture of two gases be separated? Very often this can be done by cooling the mixture. When gases are cooled enough, they turn into liquids (when a kettle boils, the steam turns back to water when it touches a cold surface). Careful cooling can be used to separate two gases unless they turn into liquids at about the same temperature. If this happens, the liquid that is formed is then distilled to separate the gases.

This method is used in the separation of oxygen and nitrogen from the air. 'Air' is a mixture of several gases, with oxygen and nitrogen as the two main ones. If air is cooled down, oxygen and nitrogen form a liquid at about −200°C (this is very cold indeed). If the mixture is slowly allowed to warm up, the nitrogen boils and turns into a gas, leaving the oxygen as a liquid.

Metals and non-metals

WHEN WE FIRST LOOK at a list of the elements we see that very few of them are liquids. Most of them are either solids or gases. The difference between liquids, solids and gases is quite easy to understand if you can think of atoms as being people. Imagine you are in a crowded room which is so full of people that you are unable to move. This is what the atoms in a solid are like. Take a few people out of the room, so that the others can move, but only by squeezing past each other. This is like atoms in a liquid. Now take out a lot more people so that everyone can move without touching each other. The atoms in a gas are like this.

The material that makes up the world is known as matter. Matter exists in either of three different forms. It is a solid, or a liquid or a gas. These are known as the three states of matter. Some substances can exist in all three forms, depending upon temperature. Sulfur, for instance, can exist as a solid, a liquid or a gas.

The way that atoms are held together decides whether a substance is a solid, liquid or a gas at normal temperatures. All metals, at normal temperatures, are solids apart from mercury. Some non-metals are solids also, but they are very different from metals. Solid non-metals are hard but brittle – they are easily shattered with a hard blow from a hammer. Metals do not break in this way but bend instead.

Atoms in metals are held together in a way that allows them to move slightly. Because of this it is possible to bend a piece of metal into a shape. Metals are used to make things which need to be strong and which require a special shape. For this reason metals are used to make things such as tools and pieces of machinery.

Metals are also useful carriers of heat and electricity from one place to another. They are called **conductors**. This is very different from the solid non-metals, such as sulfur and phosphorus. These solids melt easily and cannot conduct heat or electricity. If you try to make a piece of sulfur into a different shape, it cracks and breaks up into a coarse powder. There is very little movement possible in non-metal solids, so they cannot take any hard shocks without breaking.

Because of the way that metal atoms are bonded together, none of the metals are gases. A gas is made up of small **molecules** or atoms, and in metals the atoms are held together in huge numbers. To turn a metal into a gas, it must be heated to a very high temperature. This makes the atoms separate, but the temperature has to be very high indeed, 3 000°C in the case of iron. The non-metal solids boil much more easily (sulfur at 445°C and phosphorus at 281°C). Iodine will form a purple gas at only 183°C.

Some non-metals are gases at normal temperatures. Oxygen and nitrogen, which make up most of the air we breathe, are the best known of these. There are other gases in air and some of them are rather unusual in their

The purple vapor of the non-metal iodine is formed when solid iodine is warmed. As it condenses to form the solid again, tiny crystals of iodine are left on the cold glass of the tube.

This Etruscan gold pot with two little sphinxes on each handle dates back to 600BC. It shows how the metal gold can be beaten and shaped. Unlike iron it does not rust.

Neon is one of the noble gases. Advertising signs are often lit by neon tubes. Neon gas gives off a red light, mercury vapor a blue light, and sodium an orange light.

Because it is lighter than air, the gas hydrogen is often used to inflate the balloons bought by children at circuses and amusement parks. Hydrogen is the simplest of all the elements, and the lightest gas.

behavior. These gases are known as the noble **gases**, and they are made up of single, separate atoms. At one time it was thought that they did not make any compounds at all, and they were then called **inert gases**. Inert means that they would not react. Eventually, in 1962, scientists were able to make them form a compound with the gas fluorine, the most reactive element of all. This meant that they had to be renamed. As 'noble' had already been used to name metals such as gold and silver, which hardly react at all, the same word was used to describe these gases. Neon and argon, used in light bulbs, are two of the noble gases. Helium is another and it is used to inflate balloons, since it is a very light gas indeed. When Eddy Mercx, the famous cyclist, set the world record for the longest distance travelled in one hour, his tires were blown up with helium to save weight.

The lightest gas of all is hydrogen. This was used at one time to fill great airships, such as the Graf Zeppelin and the R100. Hydrogen burns very easily, and after several disasters airships became unpopular. Helium was tried instead,

but it is twice the density of hydrogen and cannot lift big balloons as easily.

Of all the non-metals the most common is carbon. As an element, carbon is found as charcoal, soot, graphite and diamond. Diamond and graphite are both crystals made from carbon. However, they look completely different. Diamond is not like other non-metal solids; it is one of the hardest substances known. We use it to cut and drill the hardest metals. The temperature at which it boils is over 5000°C. Graphite is black and soft. It is used as a lubricant to stop two surfaces rubbing each other away. Graphite also conducts electricity and this makes it very unusual for a non-metal.

The strangest thing about carbon is the number of compounds it can make. We know over one hundred different elements, but carbon makes more compounds than all the others put together. These compounds are often found in living things. Because of this they are called **organic** compounds. Chemists now use this word to mean carbon compounds, although many of these are man-made.

The importance of carbon

WHY DOES CARBON form so many compounds? It is the only element which can join up to form chains and rings of atoms. Each time another atom is added to the chain, a different compound is formed. Straight chains of carbon atoms can be over twenty carbons in length, and there can be several side branches. It is easy to see, therefore, how a large number of different molecules can be made up.

Each carbon atom has other atoms attached to it, and these can be atoms of different elements. The most common of these other elements is hydrogen, and the simplest of all **organic** compounds is a gas called methane. It is made of one carbon atom surrounded by four hydrogen atoms and it is found in natural gas. Crude oil, or petroleum, is made of similar, but bigger molecules.

Both methane and petroleum were formed when living material became trapped under layers of rock and mud millions of years ago. Slowly, the organic substances decayed, and changed into oil and gas. Most of the oil has been formed from the bodies of tiny animals. These were so small that you would have needed a microscope to see them clearly. Natural gas has been formed from both animal and plant remains.

Petroleum is one of our most important raw materials. When it is taken from the oilfields, petroleum has to be refined, or cleaned, before it can be used. It contains groups of compounds called fractions. These are separated by a process called distillation and each of the fractions supplies us with useful materials.

Most of the chemicals in petroleum are **hydrocarbons**. They are molecules made of hydrogen and carbon only, and it is possible to break up the larger molecules into smaller ones by a process called 'cracking'.

Using the small molecules, we can make plastics and fibres, paints and glues, and many other useful things. All this is possible because carbon is able to form chains and rings of atoms. Of course, we use a lot of petroleum and natural gas as fuels. Fuels are substances that burn, giving out heat and light. Ships, cars, heating systems, all use large amounts of our natural store of petroleum.

Carbon is also found in plants and animals. Muscle and bone both contain carbon com-

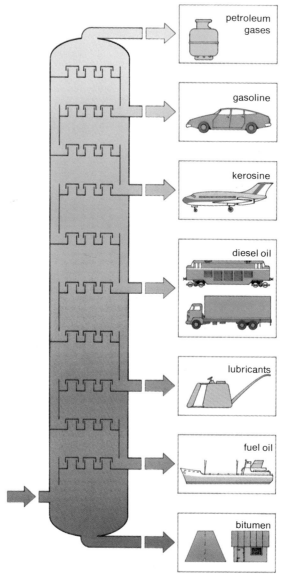

A distillation column. The crude oil is heated and the fractions separate at various levels. The lightest gas rises to the top, and the heaviest oil stays at the bottom.

pounds, as does the brain and nervous system. In fact all plant and animal tissues contain carbon. Plants contain a material called **cellulose**, and they store sugars and starch which are used to supply energy. These are all carbon compounds.

Some of the substances we can make from carbon compounds are quite unlike anything found in nature. Many of these have been made by changing natural substances slightly.

In the nineteenth century, the first moving pictures were shown by rotating a large number of glass slides in front of a lamp. Glass is heavy and fragile, so the number of slides had to be very limited. George Eastman used a clear, flexible material called cellulose nitrate as the base for the pictures, and this allowed him to roll the 'film' up. Cellulose nitrate is made from plants, and was the material which started the motion picture industry – the 'movies'. It is very easy to burn, and now the film base is cellulose acetate, a similar but safer compound. A very close relative of cellulose nitrate is nitro-cellulose – a high explosive.

If cellulose nitrate is dissolved in a special solvent, and some colored dye is added, a type of paint is formed which we still call 'cellulose' paint. This paint becomes smooth as it dries. It was first used to spray motor car bodies, to shorten the time needed for painting. Nowadays we have better materials than these, and many of these materials are called polymers.

SOME SIMPLE HYDROCARBON COMPOUNDS
There are millions of different carbon compounds. We cannot see the molecules because they are so small. Scientists need to describe them and picture them. They use a shorthand to do this, C for carbon, H for hydrogen and so on. The formula CH_4 means that the molecule contains one carbon atom and four hydrogen atoms, joined to the carbon. Molecules can also be shown as simple diagrams, or can be made into ball and stick models. The latter help us to understand that all molecules are three-dimensional, and not just flat as they appear on paper.

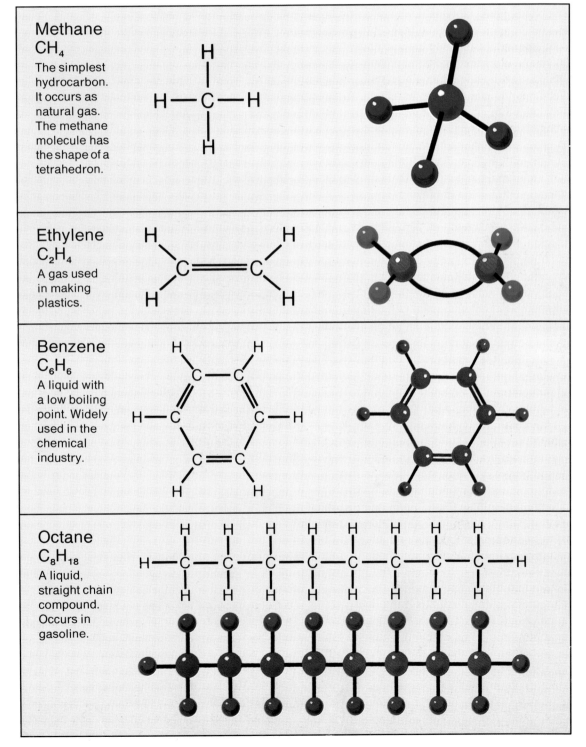

Methane CH_4
The simplest hydrocarbon. It occurs as natural gas. The methane molecule has the shape of a tetrahedron.

Ethylene C_2H_4
A gas used in making plastics.

Benzene C_6H_6
A liquid with a low boiling point. Widely used in the chemical industry.

Octane C_8H_{18}
A liquid, straight chain compound. Occurs in gasoline.

Polymers and plastics

POLYMERS have one thing in common; they are all made of very large molecules. These molecules are formed when a lot of small molecules of the same kind join together. The small molecules are known as **monomers** (from the Greek words meaning one part). They join together into long chain-like molecules called **polymers** (from the Greek, meaning many parts). You can think of a chain of paper clips as a polymer and each single paper clip as a monomer.

Many polymers occur in nature. Rubber, silk and **cellulose**, which is a part of plant stems, are all polymers. We can imitate these natural polymers, and when we do they are known as man-made or **synthetic**. The man-made polymers which we call plastics have only been in use in the last fifty years or so. Yet life without them would be very hard to imagine. Many of

Rubber is a natural polymer. The sap, called latex, is collected from the rubber trees by 'tapping'. It is shipped to manufacturers either as concentrated latex or as raw rubber.

⬤ carbon   ⬤ hydrogen

Single monomers of the gas ethylene join together to form long chain polymers. They bond together into the substance we know as polythene.

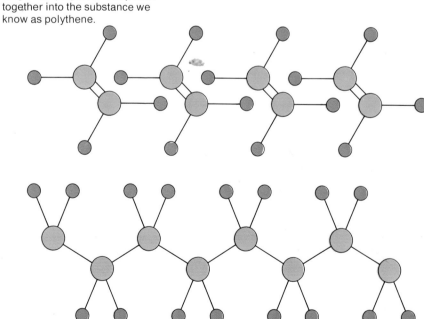

the clothes we wear contain plastics. In the kitchen you will find plastic bowls and buckets, and plastic handles on irons, saucepans and kettles.

Plastics are **versatile** materials and can be used in many ways. They do not rot or rust and they can be easily molded into any shape you want. They are light in weight but at the same time they are strong and do not quickly wear out. They can be soft and flexible, or rigid and brittle. Plastics can be made in any color, shiny or dull, transparent or **opaque**. They are also very good **insulators**. This means that they resist heat and stop the flow of electricity. For this reason, saucepan handles and the covering of electric plugs and cables are made of plastics.

Plastics are known as organic chemicals because they all contain large numbers of carbon atoms. These are usually linked to hydrogen atoms, sometimes with other atoms. Most plastics are obtained from oil. **Polythene**, for example, is made from a colorless gas called **ethylene** which comes from oil. The ethylene molecule contains two carbon and four hydrogen atoms. At least 5000 of these monomers join together to form one polymer molecule of polythene.

Plastics can be divided into two groups, **thermoplastics** and **thermosetting plastics**. This grouping depends on how they behave when they are heated. Thermoplastics become soft when heated and hard again when they are cooled. This can be repeated over and over again because the long chain-like molecules do not join up with their neighbors. They are like long pieces of spaghetti, all entangled but not joined together. **Polystyrene** was the first thermoplastic to be produced. Later polythene and PVC were developed. Nylon was produced in America by Du Pont in 1938. Since it was the joint effort of scientists working in New York and London it was named nylon (NYLon).

Because thermoplastics soften when heated and harden when cooled, we are able to make articles in a number of different ways. One process is called **injection molding**. The material is made liquid by heating and then injected in a fine spray into a mold. As it cools it hardens into the shape of the mold, forming a product such as a bowl or bucket.

Thermosetting materials soften when first heated and then harden with further heating. However, the process cannot be repeated. This is because the polymers join together, a process known as cross-linking or setting. The long chain-like molecules cross-link with each other to form one huge molecule. The first thermosetting material was developed in the United States by a Belgian chemist in 1907. His name was Leo Baekeland and the material was known by the trade name Bakelite. These materials could only be made in dark colors. Later, similar materials were produced using different chemicals so that it was possible to have a variety of colors.

Thermosetting materials are also used to make **laminates** for kitchen tops. Formica is the trade name of one laminate but there are many

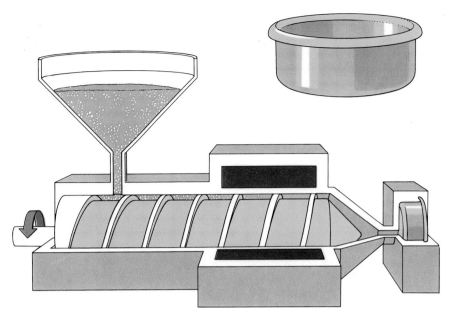

others. Laminating is like pressing a huge sandwich together. Sheets of cloth or paper are soaked with a liquid plastic. Then they are pressed together between steel plates. The heated material sets and forms a strong rigid sheet.

Boat hulls, garden pools and some car bodies can be made using fibreglass sheets laid in a mold. Polyester, with small amounts of other chemicals, is rolled into the glass fibres. After a short time the glue-like material sets and binds the fibres together. Further coats can be added to increase the thickness.

All plastic materials have one disadvantage. They do not rot, and, therefore, they give us a litter problem. One way to solve this pollution problem is to make plastics that will rot away when weather and bacteria attack them. These plastics are called **biodegradable**. Will this solve the litter problem? Paper itself is biodegradable and we still see a lot of paper litter.

Injection molding. Small plastic pellets are fed into the machine and melted. The liquid plastic is injected into a mold. The plastic is cooled and sets hard in the shape of the mold. The mold is opened and the product is removed. The process is repeated, quite fast, over and over again.

Plastics for every use

Acrylic: fibres are soft and woolly. Used for many types of clothing, sweaters and blankets. Typical trade names are Acrilan, Courtelle and Orlon. Acrylic paints are widely used.

Bakelite: first plastic to be made from chemicals. Still used for heat-proof handles on cooking utensils. Dark in color, but cheap.

Cellulose acetate: fibres used for making cloth such as Rayon, Arnel and Tricel. Also used for photographic film, and see-through windows in packaging. Used for toothbrush handles and toys.

Epoxy resins: used for very strong glues and adhesives.

Nylon: waterproof and dries quickly. Used in all kinds of clothing and carpets. Because of its strength used for parachute cords, fishing nets and tennis racket strings. In solid form, as small gear wheels and bearings.

Plexiglas: hard, tough and transparent. Used in place of glass since it is lighter and does not shatter, for example, safety goggles, contact lenses, and windows of light airplanes.

Polyesters: do not stretch or lose shape. Widely used in most textiles, for example Terylene, Dacron and Fortrel. Also used with glass fibres for boat hulls and suitcases.

Polystyrene: rather brittle and can easily crack. Much used in the kitchen for food containers and jugs, also lining of refrigerators. Can be expanded into a solid foam for use as ceiling tiles, throw-away cups and packaging.

Polythene: widely used for food storage containers, detergent bottles and plastic bags. In the form of thin film it is used for wrapping food and keeping it airtight.

PVC: short for polyvinyl chloride. It has many uses; table cloths, seat covering in cars, handbags, garden hoses, raincoats, floor tiles, guttering and piping.

Fibres and fabrics

WE USE many different kinds of fabric in our daily lives. We use them for clothing and for materials such as curtains, sheets and blankets. A **fabric** is made of **fibres** which are spun together to form a yarn. Yarns may be dyed and then knitted or woven into fabrics. The textile

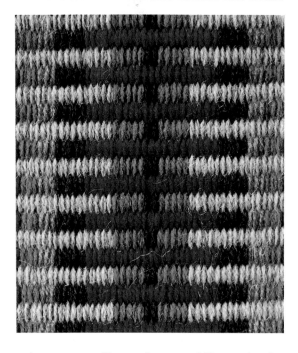

industry uses fibres of many different kinds; natural, synthetic or a mixture of both. Some have been in use for thousands of years, others have only recently been developed.

Knitting and weaving were invented more than three thousand years ago. An early form of knitting known as 'frame-knitting' was used by the Arabs. It was much the same as the 'bobbin-work' done by children today. This is the method which involves a reel or bobbin, with four nails inserted round the hole, and a system of looping movements with the yarns.

Fibres are polymers consisting of long chains of molecules. In natural fibres the length of each molecule is fixed by nature but the synthetic or man-made fibres are prepared as unbroken lengths of twisted fibre. These are called **filaments**. Before 1900 all fibres were natural, but now there are more man-made than natural fibres. Natural fibres fall into two main groups: those such as wool and silk obtained from animals and those such as cotton and linen which come from plants.

About six thousand years ago, in Central Asia, sheep's fleece was pounded with water to form a stiff matt cloth which we now call felt. Later people learned to spin the wool into yarn and then to weave the yarn into cloth. If you look at a wool fibre under a microscope you will

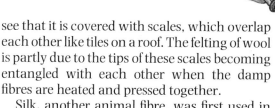

After spinning, the yarn may be dyed before it is woven into cloth on a loom. In this close-up of hand-woven cloth the warp threads run left to right and the weft threads from top to bottom.

see that it is covered with scales, which overlap each other like tiles on a roof. The felting of wool is partly due to the tips of these scales becoming entangled with each other when the damp fibres are heated and pressed together.

Silk, another animal fibre, was first used in China about four thousand years ago. Today more than half the world's silk is made in Japan.

Silk is an expensive fibre and is used to make luxury clothes such as evening gowns, scarves and ties. It is produced by an animal called the silkworm which is the caterpillar stage of a particular kind of moth. When the caterpillar is fully grown, it begins to make a **cocoon**. The Chinese call this 'a house of silk'. It takes about five days for the caterpillar to make its cocoon which is made from two silk filaments. The caterpillar has a structure on its head called a **spinneret** and it uses this to spin the cocoon. If

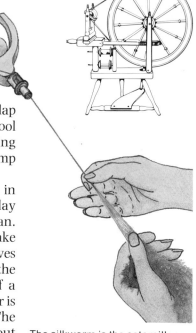

Natural fibres have to be spun into yarn before being made into cloth. This involves drawing out and twisting the fibres. Until the year 1760 spinning had to be done by hand on spinning wheels, like the one shown here.

The silkworm is the caterpillar stage of a particular kind of moth. It feeds on mulberry leaves and makes a cocoon as shown in the picture. The silk filaments are natural fibres.

the cocoon was left to develop, an adult moth would eventually hatch out. However, before this happens, the cocoon is placed in boiling water and the moth inside is killed. The filaments from several cocoons are then twisted together into a strong yarn and this is woven into silk fabric.

The method for making fibres from the seed hairs of the cotton plant was known by the ancient Egyptians and Chinese many thousands of years ago. Cotton cloth was also made in India in 3000 BC. Most of the world's cotton is grown as an annual crop in countries which have a warm, moist climate for most of the year.

The plant's creamy-white flowers turn into seed pods or **bolls**. Inside the bolls the seeds grow with long hairs attached to them. Eventually the bolls burst open and the cotton can be seen as a wad of soft fibres. The bolls are picked and the cotton fibres are removed from the seeds by machines known as cotton **gins**. They are then

Cotton plants grow best in the southern states of the United States and near rivers in India and Egypt. They need a warm, sandy soil and plenty of water. The bolls are picked by hand. Cotton is a natural fibre.

In the manufacture of rayon the natural cellulose is dissolved in an acid bath and becomes a yellow syrupy mass. The pure fibres are drawn from the bath, through spinnerets.

pressed into bales and sent to a spinning mill to be made into yarn. Linen, like cotton, is another plant fibre material. It comes from the fibres produced by the stem of the flax plant. Both linen and cotton are made from **cellulose** fibres.

The synthetic or man-made fibres also fall into two main groups. One of these groups of fibres is made completely from plastics. These include fibres such as nylon and polyester. The other group is made when natural fibres, such as cellulose, are reformed to make new fibres. **Rayon** is included in this group. Unlike natural fibres, man-made fibres are made as continuous lengths known as filaments and these may be several miles in length.

All man-made fibres are manufactured in the same way. Fibres are made up of long chains of molecules joined together. These chains are called polymers. In the first stage of manufacture, the polymer chains are turned in a syrupy liquid. The second stage is known as the spinning stage. The polymer liquid is forced through small holes in a jet called a spinneret so that the fibres appear as fine jets of liquid. These fine jets of liquid polymer now have to be hardened into fibre filaments.

In order to produce strong fibres the filaments have to be stretched. This is done while they are still soft after the spinning process. This stretching forces the long chains of molecules in the fibre to pack themselves more closely and also makes them line up along the length of the fibre. This makes the fibre stronger and helps them to withstand the pulling and stretching which takes place when they are used in our clothing. Although man-made fibres are made as continuous filaments, about half of them are chopped up into smaller lengths to make them more like natural fibres. They can then be mixed with natural fibres ready for spinning into yarn.

Inside the atom

THE CHEMIST John Dalton believed that an atom was a solid lump of matter, rather like a tiny billiard ball. Some ninety years later, in 1897, the great physicist J. J. Thomson carried out some experiments which changed the picture. He discovered that atoms contained particles with a negative charge. This type of particle was later called the electron.

We know that matter as a whole has no electrical charge. Because of this Thomson went on to suggest that atoms must also contain a positive charge to balance the negative charge of the electrons within it. However, he also thought that the positive and negative charges were evenly spread throughout the whole atom. For this reason Thomson's experiment was known as the 'plum pudding' model.

Other scientists believed that all the positive charge was to be found in a very small part of the atom, and not evenly spread as Thomson had believed. In 1911 Ernest Rutherford became the first scientist to explain the structure of the atom as we know it today.

In a famous experiment he bombarded a thin piece of gold foil with positively charged par-

Ernest Rutherford, 1871–1937, was a New Zealander by birth. It was in England that he did most of the work for which he is famous. He is best known for explaining the structure of the atom as we know it today.

ticles. Because two positive charges repel each other, these bombarding particles would be strongly deflected, or turned away, only when they passed close to regions of positive charge in the gold foil. Most of the particles would continue in a straight line through the foil. This in fact happened, and it showed Thomson's idea was incorrect. Rutherford had proved that the positive charge in each gold atom existed in only a very small part of the whole space of the atom. We call this the **nucleus**, and Rutherford showed that this occupied only about one million millionth part of the volume of the whole atom.

The nucleus of any atom is made up of **protons**, and usually some **neutrons** as well. Neutrons have a mass almost identical to the protons, but they carry no charge. The mass of a proton is nearly two thousand times that of an electron, so nearly all the mass of an atom is contained within the nucleus. The density of the nucleus is enormous, since the mass is packed into such a tiny volume. For an average atom, the density of the nucleus is about half a million metric tons per cubic millimeter.

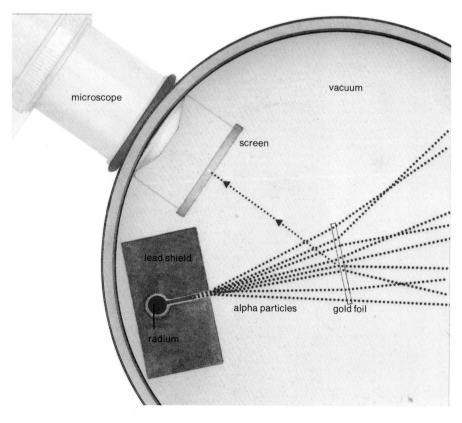

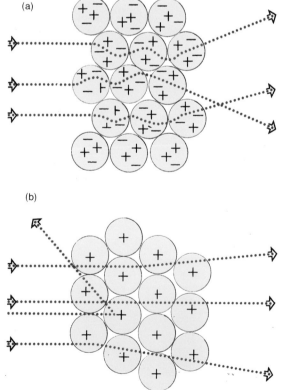

This photographic reconstruction describes an oxygen atom according to the Rutherford idea. In it you can see eight protons, eight neutrons and eight electrons. Remember that an atom is not really like this at all.

tains one orbit only, and never more than two electrons. The next shell out from the nucleus contains four orbits and up to eight electrons. The element **uranium** has a total of seven shells for its ninety-two electrons.

How atoms combine with other atoms depends on the number of electrons in the outermost shell. Those with eight, eighteen or thirty-two electrons in the outer shell are the most **stable.** They are not easily changed or broken apart. When the number is slightly less, the atom will take electrons from another atom to bring the number up to eight, eighteen or thirty-two. These outermost electrons are important since they allow atoms to combine with each other to form molecules.

A sodium atom has one electron more than a stable state of eight electrons in its outer shell, while a chlorine atom has one less. A sodium atom can therefore pass its outer electron to a chlorine atom. It becomes positively charged and the chlorine becomes negatively charged. Since unlike charges attract, the two atoms bond together to form a sodium chloride molecule. Billions of these sodium chloride molecules go to make up just one grain of common kitchen salt.

Atoms can also join together by sharing some of their electrons. This happens in the case of chlorine gas where two chlorine atoms share electrons.

The electrons in an atom orbit around the nucleus in a number of layers, called **electron shells,** at different distances from the nucleus. Each shell has a definite number of electron orbits, and no orbit can hold more than two electrons. The innermost shell of an atom con-

Rutherford's experiment *(far left)* for showing how small the nucleus of an atom is. Positive alpha particles will only bounce back from the gold foil when they strike the nucleus of a gold atom. The tiny number reflected indicates the size of the nucleus.

J. J. Thomson's theory (a) showing that the positive and negative charges in the atom were evenly distributed. If correct, the particles would alter course, none would bounce back.

Rutherford's theory (b), the correct one, showing that most alpha particles pass through the atom, very few striking the central positive nucleus.

(right) Montreal Olympic Stadium from the air. Imagine a hydrogen atom enlarged to the size of the Montreal stadium. With the single electron in orbit around the rim of the stadium, the nucleus, a single proton, would be smaller than a pea in the center of the stadium. Each atom is almost entirely empty space, with the electrons orbiting rapidly throughout its volume.

Radioactivity

J. J. THOMSON discovered that some atoms of certain elements, which seem chemically the same, have a different mass. These atoms are called **isotopes** of the element. They have the same number of protons and electrons as the ordinary atoms, but they differ in the number of neutrons in the nucleus. It is these neutrons which give the isotopes their different masses. Because a single element may have several isotopes, the total number of different types of atom is much greater than the 107 elements known. Over 1300 different types of atoms exist, and 300 of these occur naturally. The rest are made in laboratories.

Many isotopes have unstable nuclei. This means that they eject charged particles as the nucleus changes to a more stable form. The throwing out of charged particles by an unstable nucleus is called **radioactivity**, and isotopes which do this are called **radioisotopes**.

A radioisotope known as carbon-14 has been very useful to scientists studying events which took place thousands of years ago. As long as a plant or an animal is alive, the proportion of carbon-14 it contains is the same as in the surrounding air. When death occurs, no new carbon-14 is taken in. After death the carbon-14 gradually decays, or changes into nitrogen-14. Since scientists know the rate at which carbon-14 steadily decays, they can work out when death took place. They measure the proportion of carbon-14 still left in the remains of the body they are examining. In this way scientists are able to work out the age of objects up to 60,000 years old.

Medicine has found many uses for radioisotopes. A part of the human body called the thyroid gland uses the element iodine. If this gland goes wrong, doctors can inject a small amount of a radioisotope, iodine-132, into the body. The thyroid gland begins to take up this isotope. This allows the activity of the gland to be observed, by watching the build-up of radioactive iodine within the gland. Another isotope, cobalt-60, is used to treat people who have cancer. Cancer is an uncontrolled growth in a person's body, and the isotope is used to stop this growth.

Radioisotopes gradually decay, and the rate of decay is known as the **half-life**. This is the time taken for half the atoms in the isotope to break up. If the half-life is very long, then the isotope

Marie Curie, 1867–1934, in her laboratory *(opposite)*. With her husband, Pierre, she discovered the radioactive element radium, in 1898. She also discovered another radioactive element, polonium, which she named after Poland, her native land. When the Curies worked at night they often saw the radium samples glowing with a green light.

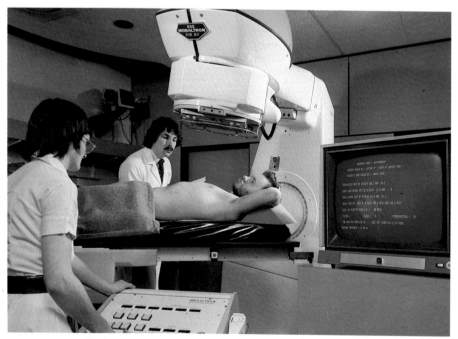

Radiation is often used to treat patients with cancer. The harmful cells can be killed with the use of isotopes such as cobalt-60. Radiotherapy is used instead of surgery when the growth is deep-rooted. The radiation is controlled by computer.

Some half-lives

Polonium	less than 1 second
Argon-41	1.8 hours
Radon	4 days
Cobalt-60	5 years
Radium	1,622 years
Carbon-14	5,736 years
Plutonium-239	24,000 years
Uranium-238	4,500,000,000 years
Lead	stable

Half-life of radioactive materials is the time taken for half the radioactivity to decay. After one half-life only half the radioactivity remains, after two half-lives only one quarter remains and so on. After ten half-lives only one-thousandth of the radioactivity remains. Radioactive elements with very short half-lives, such as polonium, disappear almost as soon as they are formed.

changes slowly. If it is short, then the radioactive decay of that isotope is rapid, which means that it is very unstable.

Some radioisotopes such as uranium emit charged particles all the time. It was a piece of material containing uranium which led Henri Becquerel to discover natural radioactivity in 1896. There are three different types of radiation given out by isotopes. The three types are called **alpha particles, beta particles** and **gamma rays.** Each of these particles is able to penetrate solid objects to a greater or lesser extent.

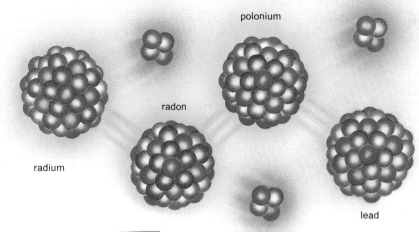

In the case of elements heavier than lead, such as radium, extra neutrons are needed to bind the nucleus together. Over a period of time the repelling force between the protons causes particles to break away. As this happens, the atoms change into those of other elements, ending with the more stable element, lead.

Alpha particles are positively charged and consist of two protons and two neutrons. They are given off by heavy elements which have too many protons to be stable. They travel at a speed of about one-twentieth the speed of light. These particles are stopped by a thickness of paper or a thin piece of aluminum foil. The

The penetrating power of radiation. Alpha particles are stopped by a sheet of paper. Beta particles pass through paper but are stopped by aluminum foil 6 mm thick. Gamma rays need a lead screen 150 mm thick to give good protection.

element radium is a source of alpha particles. It is a million times more radioactive than uranium and was discovered by Marie and Pierre Curie in 1898.

Beta particles have a negative charge. They are very fast moving electrons, which may be thrown out from the nucleus with a speed approaching that of light. They can pass through about 2 mm of aluminum. Beta particles are given off by elements which have too many neutrons to be stable, such as carbon-14 described above.

Gamma rays are often given off as well as alpha and beta particles. They travel at the speed of light, carry no charge, and have great penetrating power. A strong source of gamma rays such as a nuclear reactor needs a lead screen at least 150 mm thick for good protection.

alpha particles

beta particles

gamma rays

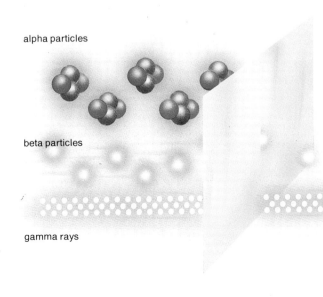

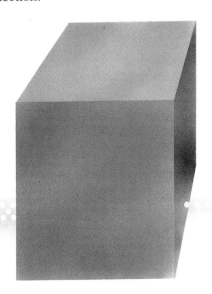

The energy of the nucleus

In 1905, Albert Einstein showed from his Theory of Relativity that only a small amount of mass could be changed into a vast amount of energy. When Einstein put forward this theory he was only twenty-six years old. Many scientists throughout the world found it difficult to believe his statements. However, Einstein's predictions came true when scientists began to investigate nuclear energy many years later. The energy from just one gram of mass would be sufficient to supply a large family with electricity for about 100,000 years.

The nucleus of a hydrogen atom consists of one particle only, a single proton. All other atoms have nuclei which are made up of varying numbers of protons and neutrons. Protons have a positive charge and neutrons no charge at all. These nuclear particles are sometimes known as **nucleons**. Since like charges repel, the protons in the nucleus are the whole time trying to push each other apart. A great deal of energy is therefore needed in the nucleus to bind the nucleons together.

Einstein had shown in his Theory of Relativity that mass and energy are related. We could say that the mass of any nucleus is made up partly of the energy that is needed to hold the nucleons together, and partly of the mass of the individual nucleons. Einstein knew that if it would be possible to 'split' an atom into smaller parts, some of this **binding energy**, as it is called, would be released.

Not all atomic nuclei are easy to break into smaller parts. Stable nuclei are more difficult to change or break apart. Physicists have shown that nuclei having between 60 and 120 protons are the most stable. An example of such a stable nucleus is that of the element iron.

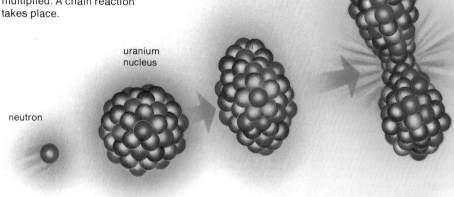

Nuclear fission takes place when an uranium atom is struck by a neutron. The uranium nucleus divides into two roughly equal parts. Two or three free neutrons are released. As they collide with other uranium atoms the process is repeated and multiplied. A chain reaction takes place.

uranium nucleus

neutron

The Oldbury nuclear power station in England. In a nuclear reactor the uranium fuel is sealed into rods. These are grouped together as fuel elements. Fission takes place and vast energy is released in the form of heat. The heat is converted into high pressure steam to drive the turbines. The chain reaction in the core of the reactor is controlled by means of rods made of a material such as boron, which absorbs the free neutrons. The reactor itself is encased in a very thick shield of concrete or steel to prevent the escape of radioactivity.

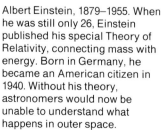

Albert Einstein, 1879–1955. When he was still only 26, Einstein published his special Theory of Relativity, connecting mass with energy. Born in Germany, he became an American citizen in 1940. Without his theory, astronomers would now be unable to understand what happens in outer space.

Nuclear **fission** is the process where a very heavy nucleus, such as **uranium**, is split into two roughly equal parts. When this happens two smaller nuclei of lighter, more stable elements are formed, and two or three neutrons are released. There will be a lot of spare binding energy and this goes to the free neutrons. This energy is the source of the heat that results from nuclear fission.

If the amount of material in which fission is taking place is small, the fast, free neutrons will escape without hitting another nucleus. But if the piece of material in which fission has taken

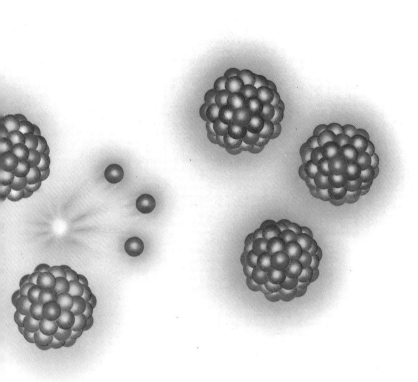

place is large enough, the free neutrons will collide with other nuclei. The process of collision is repeated and multiplied, so that a **chain reaction** builds up very rapidly indeed.

If the number and speed of the neutrons produced in the chain reaction are controlled, a steady supply of energy in the form of heat is produced. However, if the nuclear reaction is allowed to go out of control, an explosion of unbelievable force takes place. This is what happens in an atomic bomb.

In 1938, two German scientists, Hahn and Strassmann, discovered that the splitting of the uranium nucleus into two more or less equal parts would take place if it were bumped by a single, slow moving neutron. This discovery led to the development of the fission **reactor**. Various nuclear fuels are used in such a reactor. One suitable isotope is uranium-235.

In a nuclear reactor, the fast escaping neutrons are slowed down in a **moderator** made of carbon. To control a chain reaction, control rods made of boron are lowered into the atomic pile to absorb some of the neutrons and prevent the reaction going too fast. Nearly all the energy released in the process is changed into heat in the core of the reactor. This heat is converted into high pressure steam which drives the turbines in a power station. These generate the electricity which we use.

Energy may also be gained by building up a

larger nucleus from a number of lighter ones. When hydrogen atoms are combined to form helium, energy is released. This is the nuclear **fusion** process. The positively charged hydrogen nuclei repel one another strongly, so great energy is needed to fuse them together. This energy is small compared to the amount released when fusion takes place.

A nuclear explosion of immense force takes place if the chain reaction is allowed to go out of control, as in the case of an atomic bomb.

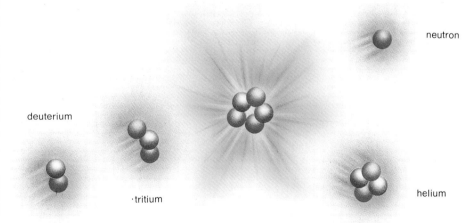

deuterium

tritium

neutron

helium

To fuse the hydrogen nuclei, a temperature of many millions of degrees is required. The process goes on continually in stars like our Sun, where the temperature is immense. If scientists could perfect this process here on Earth, we would have an unending supply of energy and most of our fuel problems would cease to exist.

Nuclear fusion takes place when two hydrogen isotopes, deuterium and tritium, collide. The protons and neutrons of the two combine, releasing great energy. The result of the explosion is one helium atom and one free neutron.

The structure of crystals

WE HAVE ALREADY SAID that a single grain of common kitchen salt is made up of billions of sodium chloride molecules. Each molecule is formed of one atom of sodium and one atom of chlorine bonded together. What is of great interest is that all these sodium chloride molecules which make up the grain of salt are not jumbled together in a haphazard way. If we could look at the atoms making up the salt grain, with a very high power microscope, we would see that they are all very neatly and carefully arranged.

Imagine you are holding a sugar lump in your hand. This is in the shape of a cube. The cube has six sides, or faces, eight corners and twelve edges. Now imagine that at each corner of the cube, and in the middle of each of the six faces, there is a chlorine atom. Then imagine that in the very center of the cube and in the middle of each of the twelve edges there is a sodium atom. What you have imagined is a single unit of what is called a sodium chloride crystal.

Most solids are made of crystals. In each crystal, the atoms are arranged in some linked and well ordered pattern just like the sodium and chlorine atoms in the salt crystal. A grain of kitchen salt consists of many billions of these crystals, stacked end to end and side by side. The distance between two atoms which are next to each other in a single crystal is only 2.8×10^{-10} m. The distance between two atoms of the same

Domestic salt crystals under the magnifying glass. Each one of these crystals may contain billions of cubic crystals of sodium chloride packed together.

kind is twice this number. This means that for your sugar lump to be the same size as a single sodium chloride crystal, you would need to shrink it so that each side of the sugar cube was only 5.6×10^{-10} m long.

The cube-shaped sodium chloride crystal just described is one of only seven ways in which crystals are shaped. The cube is one of the simplest and easiest crystals to imagine. Others are a little more complex. The interesting thing is that crystals do not grow in a haphazard way. They obey definite rules which result in the seven different crystal forms. These are all made up from different arrangements of just four basic shapes. These shapes are shown in the illustration.

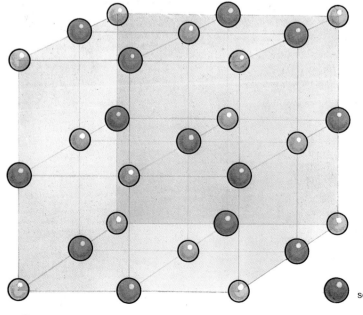

sodium   chlorine

A single unit of sodium chloride, common salt. The crystal is in the shape of a cube.

There are four basic shapes nature uses for the faces of crystals. These are the parallelogram, the equilateral triangle, the square and the regular hexagon. A parallelogram is a four-sided shape with opposite sides parallel and of equal length. An equilateral triangle has all three sides of the same length. A regular hexagon is a six-sided shape, each side being of the same length.

Cubic crystal of halite, or rock salt. A mineral found in places where shallow lakes have evaporated.

The pattern which nature creates in the snowflake crystal varies from one crystal to another. No two crystals are ever just the same, but each one has perfect symmetry. Some are star-shaped, each one having six spikes, radiating out from the center. Others are in the shape of hexagons.

Nowhere is the beauty of crystal structure better shown than in the snowflake. Snow crystals vary in size from about 0.25 mm to nearly 5 mm across. The thickness is usually one-tenth of the width. All snowflake crystals have the same basic plan. If you could examine a snow crystal under a microscope you would see that it is formed in the shape of a hexagon, or that it has six arms radiating out from the center. The angle between neighboring arms of the snowflake is always exactly the same. This is because snowflakes are made from water molecules.

Each of these water molecules contains two hydrogen atoms and one oxygen atom. Every water molecule is made up in the same way. The two hydrogen atoms form an angle of 120° where they join the one oxygen atom. This results in the hexagon structure when many water molecules join together to form a snow crystal. All snow crystals are built upon the plan of a hexagon, but the exact shape does differ from one to another. Some flakes appear as a double hexagon with twelve sides. These may be the result of two crystal growths, one on top of the other.

The hexagon pattern of snow crystals was noticed by the English scientist Robert Hooke as early as 1665. At the beginning of this century an American, Wilson Bentley, devoted his whole life to the study of snow crystals. He was entranced by their beauty, and obtained photographs of over 6000 different snow crystals. Bentley found that no two were ever exactly alike. This is remarkable when you think that during a heavy one-hour snowstorm, over one hundred billion snowflakes fall on a piece of ground about 100 m square.

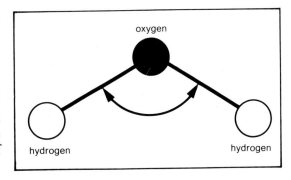

The hexagon shape of the snowflake crystal is due to the structure of water molecules. The angles of a hexagon are each 120°, and this is nearly the same as the angle made by two hydrogen atoms with the oxygen atom in a single molecule of water (H_2O).

59

Summary

IN THIS BOOK we have looked at a large number of different objects from the very smallest particles in the universe, the quarks, up to the very largest galaxies travelling in space at very fast speeds. To understand the size of many of these objects is extremely difficult. With some it is impossible. Scientists have the problem of trying to relate one thing to another. Their measurements help them to find the scale of the universe. In other words, they are able to tell how large things are, relative to one another, and how far apart they are.

Scientists need to describe the size of objects and their distances apart, using the same unit of measurement. This is a problem, because the distance between two stars is very different from that between two atoms. Suppose we chose a 1-m rule as our unit. This would be excellent for measuring the length of a football field. However, it would not be very useful for measuring the diameter of a grain of salt. Also, it would be useless for finding the distance between the Earth and the Sun.

Astronomers generally need to measure very large distances. They use a unit of measurement called the 'light-year' to do this. This is the distance covered by a ray of light, travelling at 300,000 km per second, in one year. A 'light-year' is equal to a distance of nearly 9500 billion km. The next nearest star to us, apart from our Sun, lies at a distance of about 4.25 light-years. The Andromeda Spiral galaxy,

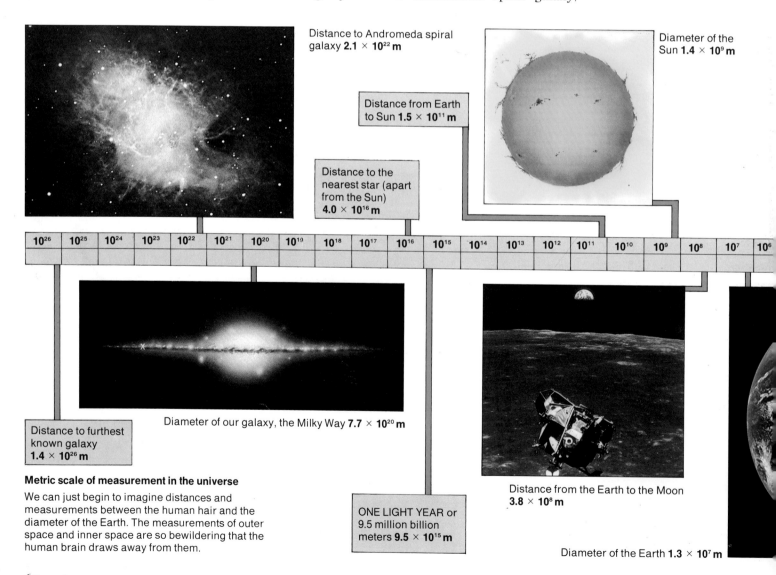

Distance to Andromeda spiral galaxy **2.1 × 10²² m**

Diameter of the Sun **1.4 × 10⁹ m**

Distance from Earth to Sun **1.5 × 10¹¹ m**

Distance to the nearest star (apart from the Sun) **4.0 × 10¹⁶ m**

10²⁶	10²⁵	10²⁴	10²³	10²²	10²¹	10²⁰	10¹⁹	10¹⁸	10¹⁷	10¹⁶	10¹⁵	10¹⁴	10¹³	10¹²	10¹¹	10¹⁰	10⁹	10⁸	10⁷	10⁶

Diameter of our galaxy, the Milky Way **7.7 × 10²⁰ m**

Distance to furthest known galaxy **1.4 × 10²⁶ m**

Metric scale of measurement in the universe

We can just begin to imagine distances and measurements between the human hair and the diameter of the Earth. The measurements of outer space and inner space are so bewildering that the human brain draws away from them.

ONE LIGHT YEAR or 9.5 million billion meters **9.5 × 10¹⁵ m**

Distance from the Earth to the Moon **3.8 × 10⁸ m**

Diameter of the Earth **1.3 × 10⁷ m**

which is the nearest large galaxy to our own Milky Way, is over 2 million light-years away. Some remote galaxies have distances of several billion light-years. The most distant object so far discovered is probably as much as 15 billion light-years from us.

In complete contrast to the astronomer, the physicist is concerned with very small objects and distances. It would be no use measuring atoms in terms of light-years. Physicists generally use the 'meter' as their unit of measurement, but add short words in front of the word meter to describe lengths much smaller than the meter itself. For example, a millimeter is one-thousandth part of a meter; milli means one-thousandth. Other dimensions used are the micrometer (one-millionth part of a meter), nanometer (one-billionth), picometer (one-million-millionth), and femtometer (one-million-billionth). A proton has a diameter of about 1 femtometer. The hydrogen atom is about 100 picometers across. A typical human hair has a thickness of 80 micrometers.

We can use the metric scale of measurement to describe lengths from the size of a proton up to the distance of the most remote galaxy known. Since the numbers are very large we use 'powers of ten', the number shorthand described on page 34.

If we say that the average length of a human stride is 1 meter we are able to express all other distances in metric terms. At one end of the scale we have the proton with a diameter of about 10^{-15} m, and at the upper end of the scale, the distance of the furthest galaxy, which may be as great as 1.4×10^{26} m.

We cannot easily understand these extremes of measurement, nor can we begin to imagine them. The table facing you contains a few examples of measurements which scientists have been able to make, using instruments or by calculation.

All we can say when we look at these numbers is that outer space and inner space are unbelievably vast and small; and that the universe consists almost entirely of space.

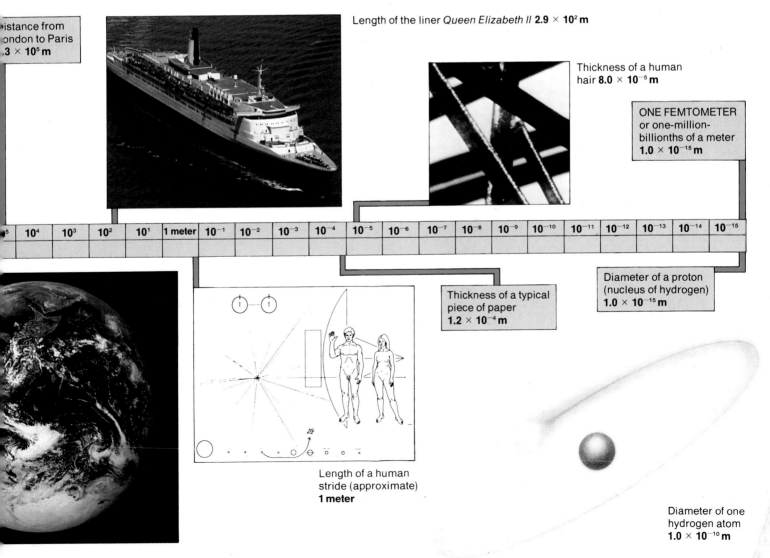

Distance from London to Paris 3×10^5 m

Length of the liner *Queen Elizabeth II* 2.9×10^2 m

Thickness of a human hair 8.0×10^{-5} m

ONE FEMTOMETER or one-million-billionths of a meter 1.0×10^{-15} m

| 10^4 | 10^3 | 10^2 | 10^1 | 1 meter | 10^{-1} | 10^{-2} | 10^{-3} | 10^{-4} | 10^{-5} | 10^{-6} | 10^{-7} | 10^{-8} | 10^{-9} | 10^{-10} | 10^{-11} | 10^{-12} | 10^{-13} | 10^{-14} | 10^{-15} |

Thickness of a typical piece of paper 1.2×10^{-4} m

Diameter of a proton (nucleus of hydrogen) 1.0×10^{-15} m

Length of a human stride (approximate) **1 meter**

Diameter of one hydrogen atom 1.0×10^{-10} m

Glossary

alchemist: a chemist of the Middle Ages. Alchemists were mainly concerned with finding a way to change other metals into gold, and with making a medicine that would stop people growing old.

alpha particle: a *particle* with a positive electric charge. It has two *protons* and two *neutrons*.

asteroid: one of many thousands of small minor planets travelling round the Sun. Most of them have *orbits* between Mars and Jupiter.

atom: the smallest *particle* of a substance that can take part in a chemical change.

atomic weight: the *mass* of an atom of one *element* as compared with another element.

beta particle: a *particle* with a negative electric charge given off by a *radioisotope*.

binding energy: the energy that holds *nucleons* together in an atom.

biodegradable: able to be rotted down by the action of bacteria.

black hole: the region left behind after an explosion in a very large star. Gravity is so great that light rays cannot escape from it.

boll: the seed-pod of the cotton plant, containing cotton fibres.

cellulose: the material that forms the walls of plant cells.

chain reaction: one event leading to another and then another, for example in *fission*.

cocoon: a case of spun threads made by an insect larva in which it changes into an adult, such as a moth.

combustion: the burning process which produces heat and light. *Oxygen* is needed for combustion to take place.

comet: a small body in the *solar system*, which sometimes has a long 'tail' made of dust and gases which reflect sunlight.

compound: a substance made up of a number of *elements*.

condense: to turn from a gas into a liquid, by cooling.

conductor: a material in which heat or an electric current can flow easily.

constellation: a pattern made by a group of stars as they are seen from Earth.

corona: the belt of gases seen as white light round the Sun during a total *eclipse*.

crater: a bowl-shaped hollow. There are many on the surface of the Moon.

crescent: the thin curved shape made by the Moon. Less than half a circle. The word comes from the Latin meaning 'to grow'. The crescent grows larger between new and half moon.

decay: to break down.

distillation, distilling: separating a mixture of liquids by heating until they become gases and then cooling. Each part of the mixture becomes liquid again at a different temperature and can be collected.

eclipse: one body in space blocking our view of another one, either partly or completely.

electron: a *particle* in an *atom*, outside the *nucleus*, with a negative electric charge.

electron shell: a layer of *electrons* circling around the *nucleus* of an *atom*.

element: a simple substance that cannot be broken down further by a chemical process.

ellipse: an oval shape. The *orbits* of the planets are ellipses.

escape velocity: the speed at which an object moves fast enough to get free from the Earth's gravity, and escapes into space.

ethylene: a gas obtained from oil, used to make *polythene* and other artificial materials.

fabric: woven or knitted cloth.

fibre: a single thin strand or thread of a material.

filament: a very long single *fibre* of *synthetic* material.

filtration: separation of a mixture of substances by adding water in which one of them dissolves and the other does not, then straining the mixture.

fission: the splitting of the *nucleus* of an *atom*. This releases a lot of energy in the form of heat.

flare: a violent explosion on the Sun's surface, sending out large amounts of energy.

focus: the point at which rays of light meet when they have been bent together by a *lens*. Also, one of two points inside an *ellipse*: a pair of lines drawn one from each focus to any point on the ellipse will always total the same length.

fusion: the formation of a new *element* by joining together light atoms such as *hydrogen*. When this happens (as in the Sun), a lot of energy is produced.

galaxy: a system of stars, planets, dust and gas forming a cluster in space. Our own galaxy is called the Milky Way.

gamma ray: harmful radiation of very short *wavelength*, that travels at the speed of light. It is given off during *radioactivity*.

gin: a machine for separating seeds from cotton *fibres* before they are spun into thread.

half life: the time taken for half the atoms in a *radioisotope* to decay.

helium: a very stable gas, lighter than air. It is the simplest element after *hydrogen*.

hydrocarbon: a chemical *compound* containing hydrogen and carbon atoms.

hydrogen: a colorless, odorless gas, lighter than air. It is the simplest *element*.

inert gases: see *noble gases*.

injection molding: shaping plastic by heating it until it is liquid and spraying it into a mold, where it cools and hardens into shape.

insulator: a material in which an electric current will not flow, or through which heat or sound waves will not easily pass.

isotope: an *atom* chemically the same as another atom of an *element*, but which has a different number of *neutrons* in its *nucleus*.

laminate: a strong, hard, protective sheet, made by bonding layers of plastic together.

lens: a piece of glass with curved surfaces which bend light to bring an image into *focus*, or to make it appear larger or smaller.

lepton: a tiny *particle*, not made up of *quarks*, which will not join to form other particles.

light-year: the distance travelled by a ray of light in one year (9.5 thousand billion km). This unit is used to measure large distances in space.

mass: the amount of material in an object. It is not the same as weight.

matter: any substance found in the universe. It cannot normally be destroyed, only changed.

metallurgist: a person who studies metals.

meteor: a small piece of *matter* travelling around the Sun. When it enters the Earth's atmosphere it burns up and is seen as a shooting star.

methane: a colorless gas, a *compound* of carbon and hydrogen.

mixture: a combination of different substances that remain chemically separate from each other. It is not the same as a compound. The air we breathe is a mixture of gases.

moderator: a material used to slow down *neutrons* in nuclear *fission*.

module: part of a space vehicle that can be separated and driven alone.

molecule: the smallest *particle* of an *element* or *compound* that can exist by itself.

monomer: a single *molecule* which will link with others to form a chain of molecules called a *polymer*.

nebula: a cloud of gas and dust in space.

neutron: a *particle* without an electric charge in the *nucleus* of an *atom*.

noble gases: *elements* such as helium, neon, and argon which do not take part in normal chemical reactions because they will not easily join with other elements. Also called inert gases. They are found in small amounts in the Earth's atmosphere.

nucleon: a *proton* or *neutron* in the *nucleus* of an *atom*.

nucleus: the central part of an *atom*, containing nearly all its *mass*.

object-glass: the *lens* in a telescope nearest to the object being looked at.

observatory: a specially designed building from which astronomers study objects in space through telescopes.

opaque: not allowing light to pass through.

orbit: the path of a body, such as a planet, around a larger body.

organic: made of carbon *compounds*, which are the basis of all living things.

oxygen: one of the gases found in air and water. It is essential to living things for breathing, and in *combustion*.

parallax: the way the position of an object appears to change against its background when you look at it from a different position.

particle: a very small piece of solid material.

periodic table: the arrangement of chemical *elements* into groups, in order of their *atomic weights*.

pharmacist: a chemist who makes medicines and drugs.

phase: the name for the different shapes of the part of the Moon that can be seen during each month. This is the part that is reflecting light from the Sun to Earth.

philosopher: a thinker, someone who thinks about how life works.

philosopher's stone: the material that *alchemists* tried to find in order to make gold from other metals.

polymer: a chain-like compound built up from a series of smaller units called *monomers*. Polymers are used in plastics.

polystyrene: a strong plastic, not harmed by moisture or many chemicals, and often used as an *insulator*.

polythene: a plastic made from a by-product of oil; used in many ways, including as protective sheeting.

proton: a particle with a positive electric charge in the *nucleus* of an *atom*.

pulsar: a very small, dense star left behind after a *supernova* explosion, which sends out regular pulses of radio energy that can be recorded.

quark: a tiny particle (not yet seen) thought to be the smallest in the universe.

quasar: a very distant and bright object, smaller than a *galaxy*, but sending out more energy.

radiation: a wave of energy such as light, heat or radio energy, sent across space.

radioactivity: the breaking down of *atoms* in some heavy *elements*. The reaction gives out dangerous *radiation*.

radioisotope: an *isotope* which gives out *radioactivity*.

rayon: an artificial fibre made from a mixture of *cellulose* materials broken down into a liquid and spun into *filaments*.

reactor: the container in a nuclear power plant in which atoms are split to produce great heat.

red giant: a star in which the supply of fuel has become low. The star's surface grows larger and cooler, but the core becomes hotter.

reflector: a telescope in which the light is reflected from a large curved mirror onto a flat mirror. The observer looks at the image on the flat mirror through an eyepiece.

refractor: a simple telescope in which rays of light pass through a lens and the image is then magnified by a second lens.

remote sensing: scanning the Earth from aircraft or *satellites* to record varying levels of *radiation*.

satellite: a body in *orbit* around a larger body in space, such as a planet. The Moon is the Earth's satellite. Artificial satellites circling Earth are used to reflect radio signals and for weather forecasting.

solar system: the Sun and the nine planets moving around it in *orbit*. The system also includes *comets*, *meteors* and *asteroids*.

spectroscope: an instrument used for breaking up light and for studying the colors of the spectrum.

spinneret: a set of small jets through which *fibres* are spun. In insects these are pores in a special organ used for spinning.

stable: steady, not easily changed.

step-rocket: a space rocket built in several sections, each of which is released when its fuel supply has been used up.

subatomic: relating to very small parts of matter, smaller than an atom.

subliming: sorting out a mixture of solid substances by heating them to change them into gases. When the gases cool different parts of the mixture can be drawn off as they become solid.

sunspot: a darker patch seen on the surface of the Sun. The surface is disturbed and has a very strong magnetic field.

supernova: a very large star destroying itself. It ends up as an expanding cloud of gas, with a *pulsar* inside it.

synthetic: artificial, made by people.

thermoplastics: plastics that soften when heated and harden again when cooled.

thermosetting plastics: plastics that soften when first heated (so that they can be molded) but also change chemically so that they will not soften when heated again.

transparent: able to be seen through clearly.

uranium: a heavy grey *radioactive* metal. It is used as fuel in nuclear *reactors*.

versatile: having many different uses.

wavelength: in wave motion, the distance between the tops of one wave and the next.

white dwarf: a very small, very dense star which has used up its nuclear energy.

Index